Executive Assistant Guide to Survival

Real Stories, Real Lessons,
Real Insights

AMAL CANDIDO

Copyright © 2020

All rights reserved. No portion of the book may be reproduced or utilized in any form or by any means, electronic or mechanical, including photocopying, recording, or by any other information storage and retrieval system, without permission in writing from the author.

DEDICATION

To my mom. You have inspired me so much to be who I am today. Your resilience and perseverance amid pain, struggles and uncertainty has no bounds. Your humility and sacrifice in all that you have done to provide for your children is a true testament and a great example to a mother's love. I am forever grateful and internally changed by all the hardship you have faced to continue moving forward in life. Your unconditional love, your unshaken faith and your vulnerabilities have inspired me deeply and touched my heart. Your love is beyond what words can describe; I can only hope to come close to being the great woman that you are! I am blessed and changed because of you. Love you forever, Mom.

To my son. Nicholas, you make me so proud to be your mom. You have grown into a wonderful young man with a compassionate heart, a great sense of humor and a passion that will carry you well through life. Every day I spend with you is always the best day ever! I am blessed to have you as my son. You have taught me all about Transformers, Pokémon, and Yokai Watch. Nothing in life is as rewarding as being part of your life and watching you grow. You are my heart, my light, and my love!

To my husband. We have been through a lot of ups and downs. I am not one to say more of the lows than the high times in life, but I must admit there is no one else I want to be with in this unsettled, rocky journey than you. You push me to my limits, because you believe in me more than I believe in myself. You see my strength and what I can do before I even see it in myself. You have seen the flaws, the hurts, and the brokenness in me, and yet you are still here. How many relationships work so well when one has fallen and the other is always there to give comfort and support? It is not great timing how that worked out. It is knowing when to stop and to lean into the struggles to make the other a priority, until we are both back on solid ground together. Agape love at it is finest! Thank you for loving me even when it's hard to "love the unlovable." I am deeply touched by the forgiveness, love, courage, and vulnerability you have shown me.

CONTENTS

PART 1
WHAT YOU SHOULD KNOW TO START

CHAPTER 1 THINGS I WISH I KNEW BEFORE STARTING MY CAREER AS AN EXECUTIVE ASSISTANT 13

CHAPTER 2 YOU WANT TO BE AN EXECUTIVE ASSISTANT? KNOW THESE SOFT SKILLS INSIDE AND OUT! 19

CHAPTER 3 THE ROOKIE EA – THOUGHTS AND TIPS TO MAKE IT THROUGH THE DAY 25

CHAPTER 4 BUILDING YOUR SELF-CONFIDENCE FROM WITHIN 31

CHAPTER 5 ONBOARDING AND OFFBOARDING PROCESS: PART 1 37

CHAPTER 6 OFFBOARDING EXPERIENCE: PART 2 . 43

CHAPTER 7 DOWNTIME TASKS FOR AN ADMINISTRATIVE ASSISTANT 53

PART 2
COMMUNICATIONS AND WORKLOAD MANAGEMENT

CHAPTER 8 INFLUENCING TECHNIQUES FOR EXECUTIVE ASSISTANTS 57

CHAPTER 9 COMPELLING COMMUNICATION STRATEGIES 63

CHAPTER 10 STRESS MANAGEMENT TECHNIQUES 69

CHAPTER 11 ARE YOU CONSTANTLY FEELING OVERWHELMED? 75

PART 3
INTIUATION AND MIND READING

CHAPTER 12 IMPROVING YOUR ABILITY TO COPE WITH JOB DEMANDS 79

CHAPTER 13 WHEN YOUR EXECUTIVE DOESN'T CARE ANYMORE – DEALING WITH APATHY 83

CHAPTER 14 WHAT YOUR EXECUTIVE ISN'T TELLING YOU 89

CHAPTER 15 AN EXECUTIVE WHO CHECKS ON TASKS THAT WERE ASSIGNED TO YOU: HOW DO YOU MANAGE? 95

PART 4
THE ELEMENTS OF TOXIC WORK ENVIRONMENT

CHAPTER 16 TWELVE EMPLOYEE TYPES THAT DRIVE YOU BONKERS 99

CHAPTER 17 WARNING SIGNS OF BULLIES AND BAD BOSSES 105

CHAPTER 18 INTIMIDATION: REFUSING & STANDING FIRM 111

CHAPTER 19 WORKPLACE CULTURES: TOXICITY AFTER A MERGER 115

CHAPTER 20 MICRO-MANAGING EFFECTS: CAN YOU CHANGE IT? 121

INTRODUCTION

I have been working for years, through high school and beyond. I was also a stay-at-home mom until it was time to put away the small toys and no longer live behind the toddler world.

Who knew that I would face biases of my own returning to the workforce after seven years, trying to convince people that I have great skills and I would like to put them into good use? It took a lot of hard work, but perseverance won, and I was ready to make the leap back in! I wanted to work with real adults and have professional conversations, using big people words! Now my work-life balance life has begun…with managing new learnings and new challenges professionally, while keeping life balance in check. Juggling home and work life have always been a delicate balance for women to maintain. It is never easy, but it has its rewards.

Now you see, I've always had an issue with separating the work-life balance "thing" when it comes to the bigger picture. You work because you have to, and you live a life at home because you want to spend time with the people you love. It's the splitting of these that I am not convinced can be done 100%, because I believe we all bring our whole self to work whether we like to admit it or not. Work is essential to building our careers. It's that part of our lives that activates passion, creativity, and a sense of accomplishment.

With that, my takeaway and learned lesson is that I need certain things from home to make my day at work easier to manage. Specifically, I need three fundamental things: mindfulness, self-reflection, and faith (or whether you want to call it, maybe hope or strength).

Mindfulness will give you the clarity to see things as they are, on the inside and outside of yourself. This clarity will help clear out the clutter and the noise around you and help you grow to be the person you were meant to be.

Self-reflection is key to living a fulfilled life, as it takes your mind off comparing your life with others around you. It will bring you to focus on your "self" to be able to answer key questions along your journey such as, am I on the right path? [your career] Who do I want to be? [your legacy] what do I want to do? [your goals or accomplishments] Where do I need to go? [your compass, your northern star, or direction]

What I know for sure is this: as much as I despise uncertainty, and even though change magnifies my fears they both played a big role in my journey personally and professionally. I was able to learn that open-mindedness will get me far in life. Having a growth mindset is crucial to succeeding whether personally or professionally. I have not completely mastered those two areas of my life. I am a working progress for sure, having yet to embrace uncertainty and change as I have always been the person who plans. That's how I measured my own success and accomplishments in general. To that end, the best advice I have ever received is to live life with intention, to hope and press through the challenges to believe in myself, to take a pause to allow for self-reflection and to live with mindfulness in order to be who I need to be.

INTRODUCTION

CHAPTER 1

THINGS I WISH I KNEW BEFORE STARTING MY CAREER AS AN EXECUTIVE ASSISTANT

I'd never thought of an executive assistant role as a career path I would be interested in. After all, when I was a child I dreamt about being a teacher, and then I wanted to be a flight attendant. When I look back, those roles always come to mind first. Once I completed high school, I found that I was drawn to travel consulting, and that was all I wanted to do. How did my childhood dreams of what I wanted to become disappear? Why did I have a change of heart?

My mother inspired me. She was a highly regarded executive assistant to the CEO of Saudi Arabian Airlines in Sudan. I guess the travel consulting and wanting to be a flight attendant was inspired by all the traveling I was exposed to as a little girl. Because of my mom's job, we traveled to many places. She even took us to the conferences she was attending for work, aside from family vacations. When I look back on those memories, they were good days, filled with warm memories of my childhood. I guess that explains the direction I was heading towards in my career. I witnessed excellence growing up; I can't say the apple fell far from the tree. All those amazing professional qualities that I admired about my mom's career inspired me to push harder, to serve with a smile, to be humble, and to share from the heart. I had learned to give more than to receive as the true meaning of hospitality toward people. In other words, I learned to be gracious and grounded.

Fast-forwarding a bit, I did end up studying travel consulting; however, by the time I graduated, my field was no longer in demand as much due to technology taking over the travel industry. With the onset of online bookings and different alternative websites available to people, there was little demand for new travel agents. I remained in hospitality though, working for airlines. That was fun for a while, but shift work took a toll on younger me and my social life, so I decided to move away from the travel and tourism industry toward something a bit more stable with daytime work. That's when my journey started in the banking industry. I was hired by temp agencies to do short-term jobs at first as a receptionist. I then moved up to an administrative assistant until I worked my way up to earn my role as an executive assistant.

Through this unplanned journey that had me land an executive assistant (EA) role; I must say I enjoy my role as an EA a lot. One might say it's my calling to be a career EA. What I noticed was that it brought together all the critical skills that I wasn't even aware I possessed: the tenacity, speed, meticulous planning, and organizing skills that drive my husband nuts, among other qualities. Who thought I would use those skills and get paid for them? The idea of it seemed so easy, right? No, I don't think so. I did not realize this journey towards building a respected brand as an EA would be a real test to my patience, strength, values, integrity, and stamina against all sorts of difficult people, scenarios, and roles. In the grand scheme of things, an EA career can be gratifying if you find the right fit and chemistry with the executive you partner with. On that note, a few things that I wish I knew before I started as EA come to mind.

> Below is a list of things that I gathered from my experience and point of view:
>
> - If you have a strong work ethic, it will scare your peers and make them look bad. They may make sure you don't shine. (This is a tough one. You are who you are, so don't change yourself to conform to the ways of others; it won't serve you well in the long run.)
>
> - If you are too approachable, pleasant, friendly, and well-dressed, you may cause animosity with the long-tenured EAs. (Find the balance for your peace of mind!)
>
> - Find a mentor immediately—someone who is seasoned and can share some guidance, wisdom, tips, and tricks of the role.
>
> - Don't follow without questioning why things are done this way or that way. Get a clear understanding of the tasks you are doing. Just because you are new to the EA role and you don't have enough experience, you are allowed to question things to get understanding. For this, you must explain yourself clearly as to why you are asking those questions. You want to avoid people mistaking them for putting up roadblocks or challenging authority.
>
> - Learn the business! Knowledge is power, and the more you know, the better you can be at your job. You will earn the respect of your peers, team members, and executives alike.

- Be curious, and don't let people slow down your curiosity; it works well with the above bullet.

- Be nice…to a point. Everyone is going to take advantage of the new person (they always do), so find the balance to learn that it's okay to say **no**. Not everyone needs to get a **yes,** all the time. Assert yourself and discern when it is a good time to do that.

- There are many politics involved. I had no idea to what degree until I lived it with each start of a new role. I knew there were politics within organizations, but I did not realize how it all played out, and how it can impact your job stability, performance, and morale. A few of my EA peers were never kind to help, support, or teach. Most of them wanted to see me fall flat on my face, so I wouldn't look better than them. Backstabbing, gossip, misinterpretation of actions, and words kept getting me in trouble. I felt that I could not trust anyone or ask for help, because even when I did, I would get in trouble. Asking for help meant I was weak and lacked knowledge. I also experienced that when people don't like your executive, they make life difficult for you too! (Keep your radar up, learn to read between the lines, and know who you can trust to be your go-to resource person.)

- Attend as many meetings as you can to ramp up quicker on getting to know the business.

- Get to know your executive's likes and dislikes quicker by asking them directly at the beginning. Don't wait to find out.

- Get involved in a professional EA community early on for training and development. You can get so much support you may not be getting from your peers within your organization. (For example, IAAP.)

- To make reasonable compensation as an executive assistant, you have to work in the C-suite level or higher (with that comes added responsibilities, having a mobile phone, being available 24/7, working longer hours; vacations and time-off are a challenge as well).

- Age discrimination and number of years' experience is a big thing (this I experienced every time; I should have listed it as number 1). "The older, the wiser" is what I was told. I have about ten years' experience in various departments and industries, but that was still looked upon as not "seasoned enough" for senior roles until I proved myself each time successfully.

- You will get no training. You either sink or swim as there is no EA manual or someone who will share their best practices with you. (Unless you work in a fantastic environment and culture that fosters such work environments, which is rare to find.) Create your manual.

- Please educate yourself that there is a difference between an executive assistant role and an administrative assistant (you can read about it by going to my website myeablog.com).

- People will always resist change, especially when a new person joins the team. The only way to work around that is to have a lot of patience and to try to understand why things are done a certain way. Determine whether it's an individual rule that is in place or company policy; there is a difference between them. Once the time is right to introduce a new process to make things easier and

> efficient, educating your team on it will be less of a struggle and something leaning more toward acceptance.

In summary, there are more items to add to this list, but then this chapter would never end! When I look back to when I started, I have had some bad experiences and have come across some evil personalities. This made me question if I wanted to continue to work in this field as an executive assistant. *Am I cut out for this? Do I have thick-enough skin?* Then I also experienced magical moments when I felt so proud of myself and my accomplishments. Executives have told me I made a huge difference supporting them, and that always made me feel so fulfilled and rewarded. In the end, it's all in the delivery. I love to build lasting connections with people I either support or work with. That brings value and meaning to the work I do, which in return brings a sense of fulfillment to me.

CHAPTER 2

YOU WANT TO BE AN EXECUTIVE ASSISTANT? KNOW THESE SOFT SKILLS INSIDE AND OUT!

You are the keeper of the keys, the holder of the knowledge. All things must pass through you! Yes, you are the incredible executive assistant. You are all things to all bosses and always there to help!

This is undoubtedly how everyone may perceive you, but in truth, you are the confidant, the business partner, and the professional problem solver/troubleshooter.

In reality, it is less flash and more substance that will give you a long career as an executive assistant. It is about dedication to the business at hand and providing solutions when needed.

There has been much talk over the years of technology replacing admins. I tend to think it's the other way around. All the technology out there helps executive admins perform their duties better than ever. Strategic counsel, event planning, project management, internal communication, etc., are all duties provided by an executive assistant, and these tasks require a human touch.

Over time, with increased responsibilities, the most demanding of roles as an executive assistant require a serious skill set. If you are committed to a career path as an executive assistant or looking to use the position to springboard to another role, there are a few skills you must get under your hat. While gaining knowledge, you will also make a significant impact and gain high credibility with your team.

Some are tangible, and some are intangible. Making the impossible possible is what you do anyway, right? Well, these are a few favorites to get you started.

Be the Calm

- If I ventured a guess, I would say your boss can be demanding, right? Their pressure, at times, will become your pressure. It's the nature of the role. This is where your ability to remain calm and to focus on the core issue helps to filter the noise standing in the way.

- Meditation, motivational prints, calming teas, noise cancelation headphones (white noise), and yoga all help build a calmer yet focused you in the office.

Be the Tech-Master...or Something Close to it

- Over time, you become the personal IT support for your executive.

- Get to know Microsoft Office (especially Outlook and PowerPoint), Google G-suite, and a few social media applications as well right off the bat. Programs like

WHAT YOU SHOULD KNOW TO START

Salesforce, ServiceNow, and travel and expense applications are used at the office and hard to gain knowledge outside of work. If you can, find someone who does use the programs and may be able to give you tips or help you become familiar with them.

- You don't have to be a Master of Technology, but you will have to deal with the time between your executive asking you to call support and the time IT shows up. This is the time your ability to troubleshoot may avert a long waiting period, and your boss can get back to work asap.

Be the Big Picture Thinker

- You are in an excellent position in the company. The perspective you have now is something very few in your company will have. Get to know your business. Once you understand both the granular flow, you will no doubt have the ability to offer a credible opinion on subject matters as requested or as an observation made to your executive.

- A great way to do this is to make a lunch date with various department heads or critical staff weekly or as needed. Don't be afraid to dig in to see what that area does and ask if they have challenges or hurdles that they wish weren't in the way. Make a few notes after lunch as your top two or three biggest takeaways. Even better is to keep these in a spreadsheet for future reference. Over time, you will have formed a foundation of knowledge and a functional understanding of the business.

Be the Gatekeeper

- Yes, this one is real to a certain degree. Keeping your boss laser-focused and organized means setting serious prioritization daily. Limiting your boss's distractions (while knowing when one is needed) is an artform to see they produce high-quality delivery to the most pressing of activities. Stand firm and be tough when needed.

- Aside from your judgment, prioritization requires collaboration with your boss; one-on-ones that include calendar, short-term, and long-term meetings, and event reviews, etc. all help here.

Be the Silent Partner

- Yes, discretion is the better part of valor. Treat everything with discretion and keep it in the vault. While transparency is the talk of business today, some matters must remain sensitive to the business and handled very discreetly.

- Trust is assumed at the beginning of your role but will still need to be earned to be effective. Keep the gossip far away and don't partake in office rumors be baited to create or comment on social media posts.

- Stuff happens, and knowing you are not perfect, you may inadvertently forward an email, or say something wrong during a conversation. If this happens, own it right away. Part of your credibility with discretion is the ability to deal with a mistake head-on rather than have it covered up only to be uncovered later.

Be the Organized One

- Yes, this does need to be said.

- Calendar management, time management, and or task management software all help here, to name a few.

Be the Multi-Tasker

- Let me say first that multi-tasking is a myth. People aren't wired to do multiple things all at once all day.

- The secret though for an executive assistant who has no choice but to try anyway is to pair basic tasks with more complex ones. Let's say you are stuck on hold; filing, doing calendar cleanup or data entry all can be done during this time..

Be the Anticipator

- Ok, this one takes a bit of time with each new role you move to, but it will eventually come. You will be able to see a few steps ahead and anticipate issues or problems in advance and be able to identify them or avoid them altogether.

- Knowing your boss's quirks and idiosyncrasies are important here. Equally important is to be able to see the business quirks and idiosyncrasies separately to understand the bigger picture in advance. I once had a boss who began to fidget about 10 minutes into our daily one-on-one meeting. While he knew the meetings were necessary, he was keen to get back to running the show. After noticing this pattern right away, I planned our meetings to focus on critical matters that took no longer than 15 minutes.

CHAPTER 3

THE ROOKIE EA – THOUGHTS AND TIPS TO MAKE IT THROUGH THE DAY

Years ago, when I started as an executive assistant, I was placed in a job by a staffing company. I was new to this role. I must admit I had no idea what to expect. For my first temporary job placement, I met with an executive who was hiring at the time. He could tell I was a rookie with no prior experience in the role before. The executive was hesitant to hire me for two reasons, one being that I had been a stay-at-home mom for the past few years, and secondly, I appeared too young. That alone was his indication that I knew nothing about the role and wouldn't be able to rise to the challenge. It is rare to ever hear "the reasons why I didn't get hired," but I was lucky enough to learn why later.

Fast forward, he ended up hiring a recommended "seasoned" EA who, as it turned out, was not a good fit and did not do a good job. As office politics go, it was one of the standard recommendations made from co-worker EAs who wanted someone they knew to be hired rather than someone most qualified.

> ***Food for Thought:*** Sometimes, it is as simple as a choice made that you had zero chance of influencing. The goal is to keep focused on the big picture and persevere. You will find something. Maybe not necessarily on your time, but keep the faith, because with your efforts, it will happen!

A few weeks later, I was called back by the recruiter, asking me if I would consider working for this executive, even though he had rejected me earlier. I needed the money, so who was I to be picky and choosy? I accepted my challenge and hoped for the best.

This experience was a fantastic entry to the world of an EA. For me, it felt like a concerted and chaotic crash course into what an executive assistant job entails. Without any guidance or prior experience or a network to lean on for resources and help (yup, it sounds crazy, as I didn't even research online to find out what was out there that could provide some sort of guidelines, tips, or tricks to support me). I was not thinking at the time. I was in the "doing and proving myself" mode.

You may wonder about the other EAs in the company—how come they did not help me? Well, I have lots of answers to that. This company had a very strange EA culture. It was not about helping each other, or sharing best practices, or helping a new fellow EA to ramp up quickly. It was more about proving they were better than YOU!

> ***Food for Thought:*** Now, I did not go in completely blind. I did have great experience in hospitality to deal with stress and the variety of personality types. Part of that background also included primary administrative duties in specific roles.

Let the show begin! Most of the EAs I interacted with were too curious about where I was before. What had I done before joining the role? How long was my contract is for? Honestly, they were too concerned with sizing me up. In the beginning, I thought to myself, "Wow, these individuals are interested to learn about me." I did not realize it was a gathering info session for them to help support the process of bringing me down.

Food for Thought: Everyone wants to impress. There will be times that you will step into roles where the "lifers" (long-tenured staff) will want to "mold" you. They will want to know everything about you and then slowly let you know how things are "done here." Your goal is to focus on your efforts to keep your boss working smoothly. Clear the noise coming from the gabby Gretas and keep moving forward.

The truth is, I am grateful for this experience, as it helped me see the good, the bad, and the ugly in a short time. I have learned so much and managed to overcome many challenges thrown my way. I earned the right to become a full-time employee from starting as a contractor. I have survived multiple companies restructures and have supported my fair share of different executives over the years.

I am standing (ok, sitting as I type this) today very proud of myself, despite some of my former colleagues who still see me as a rookie, lacking the seasonality. I have been challenged by individuals with the classic traditional mind-set of secretaries versus how the executive assistant role has evolved over the years

I was young, eager, and wanting to prove myself. My efficiency, speed, and directness, along with my friendly demeanor and willingness to be helpful, have been considered both strengths and weakness. All the extra work and owning up to my mistakes along the way add to those attributes equally. The more I accomplished, the more I ended up with more challenges, insecurities, and bad politics, and the more I faced those mind games from the gabby Gretas tearing my performance down.

If you are starting new, you need to hear about the fun and not so fun stuff. That's why I feel this chapter is worth writing about, BUT I have no intention of sharing all the ugly that I had to experience. However, what I would like to share are some of the learning tips that I have come away with.

If you are a new EA, trying to find your way and to earn the respect of colleagues alike, understand that you will meet people who will help you out, as well as people who will want to see your performance suffer to their benefit. How you navigate through all the "firsts" at the beginning of your career will determine your survival rate, learning, and building of your brand. Being an EA is such a rewarding career; however, most of you will need to go through a few valleys first before you reap the rewards.

> In conclusion, I am happy to share my thoughts and tips that helped me through it all. When you are new and trying to build your credibility, these are the things that helped and worked for me:
>
> - Understand and define your role to the success of the executive and the department you are supporting.
>
> - Get to know other executive assistants within your department/area. Find out about their experience, who they have helped or supported in the past, how long they have worked in the company, and what other tasks and duties are divided/shared among them.
>
> - Determinate if your role is over-lapping with other peers.

- Understand the expectations of the position from the executives. Determine the process of defining the role if none are in place.
- Know your executive and what works well for them.
- Don't be shy to say no (it was one of my downfalls early on).
- Build a network of EAs for support. If not possible internally, then look externally for support.
- Google is your best friend for almost everything!
- Microsoft Office and Google G-Suite are your tickets to stardom.
- Communication is your key to success; understand the different types of communication within your organization and which ones work well.
- When it comes to learning people's names, your org chart, phone directory, and global distribution lists and intranet are your guides.
- Knowledge is your power, so pace yourself and get acquainted with the company's website. Look up policies and training manuals, etc. They will come in handy in case your boss needs help.
- Identify and introduce yourself to critical individuals and partners such as finance, HR, office manager, building tenanted services, IT, receptionist, communication, help desk, direct reports and the movers and shakers within the organization, etc.
- Duties as assigned – This one is a biggie; you will find it listed in every EA job description. It is a broad statement with the possibility that "EVERYTHING" will fall

under it. So, try to get as much clarity as possible or at least a benchmark (and hope for the best!).

- Floor plan – This helps with tours and detours during your first few weeks on the job (those floor maps/plans will help you to know who sits where so you can find people easier at the beginning).

- Vacation coverage/sick days/and off-sites – What are the protocols in place? If none, create them.

- Joining meetings, managing your inbox, and scheduling one-on-ones are very important in establishing and creating great work habits, opportunities for learning, and relationship building with your executive.

- Observation, active listening skills, and even more observation are the powerful skills that have helped me succeed time and time again. They became my key strengths that I was able to develop well over time.

- There are plenty of strategies that work best and are not included in the list above. Best of luck to all the new executive assistants out there. Be brave, stay calm, remain confident in your ability, stay humble, and decide what your brand is and build it with grace.

CHAPTER 4

BUILDING YOUR SELF-CONFIDENCE FROM WITHIN

Most people, at one time or another, tend to struggle with self-confidence. Some don't even realize how much they struggle with self-esteem until they find themselves questioning why they are continually stuck in a rut.

Lack of self-confidence shows up in different scenarios or forms in our lives. A few are listed here:

- At work during meetings, when you are not feeling confident to speak on a topic you knew well
- Social events or professional networking events
- Conferences, forums, seminars
- Appearance and comfort within your skin
- Language barriers
- Expecting perfection (putting pressure on yourself)

- Relationships

- Your community, family, or friends

- Status—social, economic, or other

The list could go on, but I am sure you see where I am going with this. When you lack self-confidence, 9 out of 10 times, it comes from a place of insecurity deep within. This means it requires effort to self-check and to get to the root cause of it. Building yourself up is the key to self-confidence, versus relying on other people in your life to help you build it. It starts by internally understanding yourself and how you feel about yourself. It's more important to self-check how you view yourself than how others perceive you. Behaviors that contribute or enable the lack of confidence in you or in your life should be identified during your self-check. Are the people who surround you building you up, or are they tearing you down? Do you have people whom you trust? Or are they critical with your appearance, relationships, decisions, success, failures, or mistakes you've made along the way? There are many of these external and internal forces that apply. The key is to quiet down the noise to filter the side effects of what is causing your lack of self-confidence at this time.

Once you figure out the factors that are related to your lack of confidence, you can then start to learn how to build your confidence from within. I am not an expert on the subject, given I suffer from a lack of self-confidence as well. However, I have learned to recognize the voices and thoughts in my head that bring all sorts of put-downs, and I started to self-talk with myself to stop the noise and to get real about thoughts in my head.

Here are a few things I do personally to build my self-confidence within:

- Read books that inspire me, on topics that most people don't like to talk about (**Brené Brown** books are great!)
- Watch Oprah's "Super Soul Sunday."
- Listen to uplifting music. It's good for the soul and the spirit.
- Do meditation geared specifically towards self-love, self-confidence, and loving-kindness.
- Dedicate time on the weekend to take care of myself (getting a haircut or color, a facial, a new outfit, or my nails done, etc.).
- Surround myself with a circle of friends whom I trust, admire, and enjoy their company and wisdom in my life.
- Turn to God. When all else fails, God is my soft place; in the stillness, when I turn to his scriptures, my heavenly Father always reminds me that He is pleased with what He created. I am created in His image with unconditional love, mercy, and grace.
- Empower myself with knowledge, sometimes specific, sometimes general.
- Do acts of bravery daily.
- Dress nicely, putting on heels and makeup. It's a real transformation that has a "feel good" effect in an instant.
- Be grateful.
- Smile a lot.
- Know my values and principles and live by them.
- Organize and plan things. Order is essential in my life as it helps me feel in control.

- Exercise.

- Enjoy time with friends and family (people in your life who cheer you on and love you).

- Eat healthy and take pride in keeping a healthy weight.

- Enjoy being in the presence of nature. It gives me the feeling of fullness, calm and joy.

- Know my self-worth; this should never be determined by anyone else's opinion.

- There's no need to shrink yourself for other people's comfort.

- Know that my strength will sometimes be viewed as weakness: many people believe that kindness, emotion, and vulnerability aren't necessary (or even appropriate) in the modern workplace. Some people also view these actions as signs of weakness. But mentally strong women understand that these can all be signs that you are mentally stronger than most. Mentally strong women stay focused on growing stronger and becoming better, regardless of what their critics say. There's no need for them to prove their inner strength to anyone else for attention. They recognize that their strength will likely remind others of their weaknesses.

- Mental strength can be contagious: mental toughness isn't something you can force on anyone. But your desire to grow stronger and become better can inspire others. Mentally strong women know that strength has a ripple effect, yet they don't lecture, or beg people to change. Instead, they lead by example. And their energy in creating the strongest version of themselves often inspires others to follow their lead.

- I can't always see inner strength. Mentally strong women know that you can't judge someone's strength by the actions you see. Therefore, they aren't concerned about showing off their mental muscles. Instead, they work on growing better with little concern about whether others recognize or applaud their growth.

- Mental muscles must continuously be maintained: That means you must continually work on giving up bad habits that threaten your mental strength and develop healthier habits that help you keep growing stronger in the effort to reach your highest potential.

Finally, believe in yourself (here is where the self-talk happens for me). I get into a dialogue with God, reaffirming God's plans for me and my life, knowing that I am created with a plan, and God is willing to utilize those skills and talents for his glory. I am a disciple in the making!

If my world gets messy and chaos abounds, getting rid of the clutter in my home, work or life helps me feel in control as my self-confidence thrives on organization and planning. It is the calm in the center of the storm that makes all the difference.

Somehow, I can't believe that any heights can't be scaled by a man who knows the secrets of making dreams come true. This special secret, it seems to me, can be summarized in four Cs. They are curiosity, confidence, courage, and constancy, and the greatest of all is confidence. When you believe in a thing, believe in it all the way, implicitly and unquestionably. – **Walt Disney**

Leaving you with a motto, I aspire to live by daily…...

> I am in competition with no one. I have no desire to play the game of being better than anyone. I am simply trying to be better than the person I was yesterday.

CHAPTER 5

ONBOARDING AND OFFBOARDING PROCESS: PART 1

Does Quality Experience Matter?

This is a topic close to my heart. Why? Unfortunately, I am speaking from real-life experiences where I have been at both ends. I've been the person who was new to joining an organization/department (onboarding) and the person leaving an organization or as a witness to a release of an employee.

I must admit that some of the decisions I've made when leaving an organization were due to first impressions I had received and a general lack of welcome I felt in my first few weeks in the new role. It was a clear indication for me to realize that it was not a good culture fit.

It matters how the people you work with, report to, or the ones you come across within the workplace treat you when you are entering or exiting an organization. It says a lot about the culture of that organization and how engrained it is.

Whether you are a hiring manager, the employee, or an HR person involved in dealing with the onboarding or off-boarding process of the line of business you support, you really must ask yourself a few crucial questions.

To build world-class organizations, a company must foster a culture of quality, connection, and intent. The first place to review how you can get there or maintain such an environment is by starting with the onboarding experience a company provides for new hires as well as for employees who either choose to leave the organization or are being released.

How you treat your employees entering as new hires to the workforce or leaving your company matters, as it will reflect on the company brand, what it represents and how it stacks up against the "Best Places to Work" ratings.

It does not take a lot of effort to do the right thing. If the culture of the organization lives and breathes their values and mission statements, has the right people in place and works to maintain their status, they are naturally getting to a better-quality experience for future employees.

I am going to tackle onboarding as part of this chapter. This starts from the initial phone call to scheduling an interview, the face-to-face meeting, and finally, from the offer letter to the first day. These steps are leading to the candidate joining the company and to every interaction along the way. Just as companies like to be impressed by the candidate, so do the potential candidates themselves. They also have a stake as well in investing their career, skills, and talents where they will be valued, respected, and appreciated.

So, what happens next? On the first day or a couple of weeks, it's critical to establishing a long-term commitment and positive results from the new-hire prospective.

WHAT YOU SHOULD KNOW TO START

- Create a schedule for the first two weeks with introduction meetings. These can be with business partners across different departments to help build support working in a cross-functional team environment.

- The expectation of roles and responsibilities should be clear from the start. The new hire should have a clear direction and line of sight on what is expected.

- A welcome lunch is a great start, when possible.

- Have introductory meetings with colleagues within the team that they will work with. The new hire can then understand who does what. This is an excellent opportunity to place a face to a name.

- Give them a tour of the office, so they can have a sense of direction of where the kitchen, washroom, printer room, other team members, and meeting rooms are and where to pick up their mail.

- Provide a dedicated work area for them that is fully equipped and ready to go. This should include at a minimum computer equipment, phone, name tag, and necessary office supplies.

- Schedule time with the new hire, to help them navigate and familiarize themselves with internal systems, websites, and where to find or search for necessary information.

- Provide essential phone numbers such as IT support, HR help desk, payroll and benefits, mailroom, building security and maintenance, etc. These are all useful resources for the new hire to manage and troubleshoot on their own, when/if issues arise.

- To impress a new hire on their first day, give them a welcome package that's nicely done, including all the vital information listed above.

- Their "welcome kit" should include: a notebook, pen, coffee mug, reusable water bottle, a copy of the company core values, mission statement, code of conduct, a phone directory with the numbers that may need to be highlighted, a company-branded pin, an emergency exit procedure, etc.

To summarize, there are many ways to make your new hire feel welcome and to fit in with their new environment. I cannot stress enough how important it is for companies and HR departments to enhance the experience of onboarding for new employees. Involving executive assistants to help support this process is critical to the success of the onboarding experience. By utilizing the knowledge and the expertise of the executive assistant, it's essential in creating a great "first impression" and a unique, personalized, world-class welcome experience.

To be a world-class organization that attracts and retains top talent, you must treat them as such. Your employees are your most valuable assets to your success, creating a culture and brand that every company will envy.

As I mentioned early on at the beginning of this chapter, from personal experience, I have left companies due to poor experience and treatment throughout the onboarding process and beyond. Those are the alarming signs that new hires look for, and if the onboarding was a turn-off, it sets the stage for the longevity and loyalty of the new employee towards the organization.

To that end, in the next chapter, I will be writing about the off-boarding experience, so stay tuned for the next chapter following this one.

CHAPTER 6

OFFBOARDING EXPERIENCE: PART 2

In my previous section, I spent time addressing the onboarding process and experience for new hires joining organizations. With that said, this chapter will be all about how gracefully companies need to learn to exit employees with respect and dignity (offboarding). The quality and experience of that step are essential, especially for employees who have worked and served the company for an extended period.

Once again, from personal experience, I have witnessed long-tenured employees exiting companies due to the restructuring of internal departments, due to new leadership coming in place that created a ripple effect across departments, or due to cost-cutting. I was also the one who resigned and left a department or an organization. Although the choice of leaving was my own, I had to bear the retaliation treatment of making such a decision during my two weeks' notice as the standard professional thing to do when you resign from a job.

So, why does the off-boarding experience seem so awkward? How does one eliminate the awkwardness, take away the bitter emotions and create a smooth, graceful exit when companies and employees cut ties or vice versa?

The answer is simple: the reality is employees and companies deciding to break the relationship is not an easy decision. Emotions will always run high; employees will experience going through the five stages of grief. One day, they will feel okay; the next, bitterness sets in, or sadness, or happiness in seeking a new adventure, etc. The key for both sides is to handle this well, with the professionalism that matters to your brand, whether that is of the company or the employee who is leaving.

That said, what should happen if an employee decided to leave the company on their own on good terms? The steps involved following their notice and last days remaining to serve their resignation notice can help their department, manager, or team members with the workload and leaving a lasting positive impression.

- The first step is the employee serves their notice via written letter in person and via email for documentation purposes.

- The manager should handle communication announcement or if the employee has direct reports, it should be communicated to the team or department.

- If the role needs to be filled, an HR consultant or recruiter supporting the line of business should immediately be notified to post the position

- Before posting the position, job descriptions need to be revisited, and understanding of roles and responsibilities and expectations of the structure need to be reviewed. This is where the hiring manager has the chance to update what the role does or create new sets of responsibilities to adjust the position for future business demands and to stay competitive in the market.

- Once you take the time to review the job descriptions and determine compensation, you are ready to post the position.

- The departing employee should immediately create a list of projects or items they were working on with specific details of milestones ahead. These deadlines still need to be met.

- The employee should begin clearing out their desk and files in case this has not been done or maintained over time.

- Exiting employees could gracefully offer to help with job description feedback, or screening interviews if time allows and if the hiring manager values their input in the process.

- The employee will start getting busy with tying loose ends and saying their goodbyes to business partners and colleagues.

- The employee may be invited to coffee meetings and lunches with team members they have worked very closely with, leading up to the last day for a final get together with the whole department.

- The employee may need to have a final update meeting with their manager in the event the new replacement was not hired by then, for the manager to understand what is pending.

- The exiting employee should hand over their pass card access, keys to their desk, a list with any applications and shared folders they have access to, company phone, and corporate cards, and they should submit a final expense report to close the account and return equipment to the hiring manager.

In a perfect world, the points listed above would make a tremendous offboarding experience when exiting a company on your terms.

However, what happens when someone is forced to leave? Do the above-listed points take place? Unfortunately, no. The experience is quite different.

There is secrecy involved. The employee may sense changes in the air and may not be sure what is happening around them. They may have a gut feeling something is happening, but not confident of what or why.

The employee may notice a change in the manager's behavior, frequent HR meetings, and closed-door discussions. The employee may notice many questions regarding projects or other items and tasks that suddenly were not of interest to the manager. Still, somehow, it became necessary to them now.

Perhaps it's a meeting with the employee to find out where they are with tasks and being asked what projects they are working on and to provide a list. The employee may notice slowly that the manager is removing tasks, responsibilities, and projects from the employee and giving them to others on the team. When confronted and asked by the employee on the recent changes, management may drum up justification regarding new strategies or a shift in focus, etc.

At this point, it does not matter for what reasons companies make those decisions on offboarding an employee. You can't change the reasons, mainly if they are guided by cost-cutting or a change in leadership. We all know that those reasons cannot be reversed for the most part. But that is not what I want to address; I want to discuss how companies can treat those employees they are releasing with dignity and respect, as it matters to both sides.

So, then what should happen when decisions are made at the management level with the help of HR:

- An early morning meeting is scheduled with the employee to terminate (it's ALWAYS been the case). It's the first sign that the employee knows once they walk into that meeting room, it's the end of the line for them. Can this be handled better? Maybe, by choosing a different time or allowing the employee to say goodbye to their team members and to gather their things. That would be a good start (provided the employee does not pose a behavioral concern). Employers might not change the time of the scheduled meeting, but to release with respect and grace, you should allow the employee to gather their belongings and say their goodbyes to their team. How to do that? Simple: during the terminating meeting, make arrangements and agree with the employee and HR rep that they are allowed to go back to their desk. In contrast, the HR rep is present, to gather their items and say their goodbyes quietly, with very little info to be told in front of the team.

- One way to handle the team goodbye for a leader is by HR gathering the team in a meeting room while the employee is packing. Once they are done, they join the group by making a few remarks (agreed in advance). "They have decided to pursue other career opportunities, and they would like to say their goodbyes and to thank the team for all their support during their time here." It's about preparing a speech, but rather than the manager or HR giving that speech, you allow the exiting employee the opportunity to do it. Note: Most companies are advised by HR not to let a released employee have interaction as they walk out the door to avoid a meltdown or negative employee behavior. I believe if the delivery and representation of the company when releasing an employee is respectful, compassionate and kind, you won't have to fear those sorts of outbreaks (it's all in the delivery, so learn to be a good steward of kindness in your approach as these are people's lives you are dealing with).

- In addition to the payment owed to the offboarding employee, it helps to offer out-placement support for four months to help the exiting employee with job search, resume, and interview techniques.

- Offering a list of networks for them to reach out, to soften the blow, helps.

- Provide a letter of recommendation. For the love of God, they must have done something right for your company, so do not release them empty-handed. For those tenured employees, who served the company for many years, give them what they deserve.

- Don't make it personal. If you know they are good workers overall, but you disagreed on their style of work or management, don't treat the exit as an opportunity to stick it to the employee. Just do the right thing and take retaliation out of the equation. That goes for all levels, whether the manager or HR and the employee were not getting along personality-wise, but the work ethic was strong. Do the right thing "at the forefront" of everything you do!

WHAT YOU SHOULD KNOW TO START

- Have a termination checklist of items that need to be returned or removed. While you are having that meeting, you should have already notified the EA, IT, payroll and benefits, to coordinate a proper, respectful release of the employee (some companies will do this step after they release the employee, which does not feel good for the employee as it causes so much confusion and stress). You don't want to add to their stress and anxiety at the time you are releasing them.

- Granted, there are cases where, for security reasons, you must release and let go of the employee immediately. That all depends on two reasons: what damage they have done to the company or the type of position and access they have. For obvious reasons, it's HR and the legal department's responsibility to protect the company from any further damage to its brand and reputation and to secure their clients or company information.

- I know there are costs to this service, but if you know the employee is decent, loyal, and with high integrity, you can help show the value you had for that employee in what they represent by at least offering a counseling service for job loss. Most companies have those in place as part of the benefits of the employee assistant programs. Your HR rep could arrange for counseling for the exiting employee to help support and manage their job loss for 4 to 6 months. It will make all the difference to the employee and to their family. You are saving face with grace!

- The same goes for medical coverage; if you could arrange for four months, that would also go a long way. It's a huge gesture of good faith!

To summarize the off-boarding experience, don't we all deserve to be treated with respect, even if personalities or performance were not on the same page? The opposite of this is to feel as if you are a real criminal to be treated, walked out, and released in such a manner.

Companies have a lot to lose as these offboarding employees will share their experience and accounts of their release in social media and their network that may hinder the brand and reputation of the company. (Companies like Glassdoor allow for anonymous postings for those concerned by an NDA.)

The exiting employees will still be in contact with a few internal current employees. They would share the details of their experience with the existing employees, where it may create shock and mistrust between current employees and the company if the experience was terrible.

The mentality of "everyone's replaceable, we are all numbers, it's business" is as strong today as it ever was. Your current employees will doubt your leadership, your value, and what is important in silence, which, in turn, will create a culture that puts their guard up and their armor high. You lose morale and connectivity, and an uptick in gossip begins due to a lack of transparency.

Companies cannot mess up with onboarding or offboarding, as a lot is riding on those two steps. I hope that in the future, this will evolve and change to create a quality experience on both sides, with companies and HR spending more time understanding and working towards better-quality experiences for their employees, not just their clients.

Everyone matters; it depends on how much you care and what values you stand for. What will your legacy be? How will you impact the world around you.? Mindfulness is the key to understanding all that is involved with a clear lens to create a ripple effect of kindness, compassion, and empathy in your approach.

CHAPTER 7

DOWNTIME TASKS FOR AN ADMINISTRATIVE ASSISTANT

We don't always have the time to do things that we want to. However, one piece of advice I found that works for me is when I have downtime at work, I find something to do. I don't sit idle! I am about to share some of the things I tend to find for myself to do to keep day busy and productive:

- *Clean Up/Re-Organize My Desk*

I go through my whole desk and clean out the inevitable paper files, move things around to make them more accessible, and toss out old pens that don't write. I clean my keyboard, monitor, chair, and phone (in my experience, these always need cleaning). I get rid of the dust from my keyboard tray. In other words, I bring everything back up to shine (or as close to it as you can) and make everything nice and organized.

- *Review My Files*

I go through and review my files. I start with my working files/follow-up/or pending files to make sure everything is current and appropriately labeled. I also make sure labels and records are in good condition and do not need to be replaced. I remove files that are no longer current to reference/historical files. I do the same thing for my main files, moving older items to archives. You can create a reference chart when you're looking for a file but can't remember where you filed it (that's saved me a lot of time searching for it).

- *Read Through My Contacts*

Whether you keep them in hard copy in a Rolodex or electronically in a program like MS Outlook (that's how I keep them), periodically review your contacts and update the information. I'm not just talking about phone numbers and addresses, but also little details I learn over time like the assistant's name and number (vital information), spouse and children's names, likes, and dislikes. Also, any negatives that you might need to know about next time they visit or call. These are the kinds of details that help build connections and relationships, making people/clients feel appreciated.

- *Review My Desk Reference/Procedures Manual*

I go through my desk reference/ procedures manual and look for items that need updating or adding. Have you taken on an adjusted or new duty that has yet to be documented? Have some of your functions changed over time? Take time to update your desk manual in case you move on to a new role so the person coming in to replace you knows how things are done. This also helps speed up the ramp-up time and the time it takes training them. If you don't have a desk reference manual, this is the perfect time to make one, isn't it?

- *Organize Office Supplies*

It's been my experience that it doesn't matter how often you organize your office supplies. They always need straightening again. I don't know what it is, but when people get into the office supply cabinet, they are like little kids, just scattering things around. Straightening up the office supply cabinet is always good for a few minute's works when you're at loose ends, and people notice and appreciate when the supply cabinet is user-friendly.

- *Set Up Recurring Tasks*

I went into MS Outlook and set up recurring task reminders for all my daily, weekly, monthly, and yearly duties. I use color coding and customs flags on items that are highly important for follow-up in the future. That way, when days are crazy, it's easy to remember tasks that might otherwise slip my mind. I have reminders set up for everything from remembering to lock my cabinets before I leave, to big things like running year-end reports. While I don't need the reminders every day for everything, it's nice to have them there on those days that I may forget.

- *Review of Office Equipment*

If some of my office equipment is aging, if I need an upgrade to MS, if my printer need a new toner, or if my executive's mobile phone is up for an upgrade, I spend some time looking at processes/steps and alternatives, so when I do need to replace some of our equipment, I can do so quickly and easily.

- *Redesign Reports*

I take the opportunity to redesign reports, especially with regular reports that I look at and think could be done better but I just never had the time. Nothing like the current free time to do so. I start re-designing some of those reports that have useful information but are ugly to look at or the ones that have valuable information but could be concise. I like to keep a list of these little projects to have around for when things slow down. It gives me time for innovation and creativity.

- **Enter Business Cards into Contacts**

Usually, my boss will have a huge stack of business cards that he is hoarding; I enter them into his contacts list in Outlook. If you have a business card scanner, that makes it even more efficient.

- **Brush Up on My Software Skills**

The amount of software skills an excellent administrative assistant is expected to know is mind-boggling. To put it simply, I use my downtime to increase my ability with existing software or even to expand my skills with new software. You'd be surprised how much using the help feature alone in a program teaches new things.

Nothing looks worse for an administrative assistant than to be seen sitting idle. Regardless of how much work you do, showing initiative is very important, trust me. What they'll remember at review time was the one time they saw you sitting with nothing to do.

CHAPTER 8

INFLUENCING TECHNIQUES FOR EXECUTIVE ASSISTANTS

There are definitely some challenges that executive assistants face in their roles. One of the most common challenges I have personally experienced is influencing without authority with a team or direct reports to the executive.

I have read a lot of material on the topic of influencing without authority, as well as having attended workshops that provided a deep dive into the subject. Hopefully, what I've gathered and understood will benefit you. It's not easy to try to convince a group of people or a team you work with on recommendations or directions without the authority behind your title. It's a fact some will respect your insights and trust them. Others will try and pull the rug from under you using roadblocks, negativity, or everyday outright resistance to new ideas and change.

The Six Top Challenges that Prevent Influencing Successfully:

1. Lack of authority
2. Perceived credibility
3. Administrative/operational vs. business mindset
4. Self-limiting obstacles
5. Lack of practice
6. Lack of support from the executives

However, despite the challenges listed above, there are opportunities that an executive assistant can utilize to influence their audience:

1. Change of leadership
2. Credibility and image
3. Increased fluency and confidence
4. New alliances and networks
5. Increased productivity

Influencing, as a mindset, is different than informing. Influencing is a deliberate process of persuasion with goals. This requires understanding why the other person could say no for you to get them to yes. That's where empathy is essential; you do not have to agree but just understand the other person's point of view. If you think you can't, you won't!

There are a few extracts from author Dr. Karen Keller included below. I have personally come across items on this list at one point or another. These are the top unique traits of effective influencers:

- They do not overwhelm the people they attempt to influence with too much information.

- They use a deliberate, systematic influencing process based on position or interest-based appeals.

- They have a clear influencing goal: awareness, interest, commitment, and action.

- PASSION is the fire in their spirit for what they do. The expression of their enthusiasm and their eagerness starts the engine for their success.

- TRUSTWORTHINESS is a high virtue and is self-explanatory. It is worth noting that of all the influence traits, this is usually the most crucial. Lose trust, and influence is instantly lost.

- LIKABILITY is more than being friendly. It's their capacity to create positive attitudes in the people around them, focusing those attitudes towards a common goal.

- COURAGE is their strength to face difficult circumstances (or even difficult people) head-on.

- CONFIDENCE has a "whatever it takes" attitude. It's their mental attitude of believing in, trusting in, and relying on themselves and their abilities.

Influencing on positions versus interests: Positions are tangible things people say they want (e.g., money, budget, ROI, resources, deadlines, contracts, bureaucracy, policies, etc.). Interests are the more intangible motivations (e.g., credibility, recognition, teamwork, efficiency, financial stability, fear, pride, security, belonging, quality, fairness, etc.). While the two influencing attributes of positions versus interests exist separately, the solution on the direction of influencing is generally the same.

- You must identify the issue and its impact/risk to the department or organization.

- You must present the benefit (gains or vision) of an alternative outcome.

- You must submit your recommendation to achieve the alternative outcome.

To manage a good outcome while influencing your team or executive, it is ideal to generate options by asking "what if..." This is helpful for proposing options and considering benchmarking to adapt ideas from others. Propose a trial or test as an option to gain experience and buy-in from others. Reframe a problem as an opportunity. Share some tips on overcoming resistance with others as you practice your influencing abilities.

The goal is to enhance one's current fluency to progress to the next level of competency, confidence, and commitment with that in mind:

- Don't take it personally.

- See objections as opportunities to learn.

- Use the power of silence.

- Use the power of questions.

- Collect small yes's based on mutual interests to build trust and ownership.

- Find the strength within your resistance.

- Learn to be more open and flexible.

- Highlight the ups of the change.

- Realize people don't fear change; they fear the loss of the status quo.

- Divide to conquer.

COMMUNICATIONS AND WORKLOAD MANAGEMENT

- Communicate.
- Inspire.
- Engage, inform, explain, empower, and reward.

Knowing others is intelligence; knowing yourself is true wisdom. Mastering others is strength; mastering yourself is real power.
— **Lao Tzu, Tao Te Ching**

CHAPTER 9

COMPELLING COMMUNICATION STRATEGIES

Recently, I took an online course in communication. Through it, I learned how to use four simple strategies to communicate in the workplace professionally. I could not believe how simple yet easy those four strategies are, and the question I asked myself was, "How come I never thought about that? How can I use them now?"

After the course was over, I managed to put the strategies to the test. When conflict did arise at work, the results where amazing. I was able to cool the situation and communicate in a compelling way, especially when the stakes were high for both sides. You will find them helpful no matter what your style, or your communication partner's style, might be. Let's dive into the topic a little be more.

What a Communication Strategy Is and Isn't

Communication strategies are not about coercive manipulation or "tricky" office politics. It's essential to recognize that manipulation happens all the time. It's a reality of any interaction between two or more people. However, it's different within the office environment for two primary reasons.

First, we seldom, if ever, like everyone we work with. Our co-workers and managers aren't necessarily people we would choose to spend time with outside the office. Some of them may even hold values that are significantly opposed to ours.

Secondly, we have minimal choice about whether to be with these people. Our livelihood depends upon our showing up at work every day and doing our best to get along with everyone in a cooperative, collaborative fashion. Because of these reasons, the experience of negotiation, and strategic communication in general, often feels very different in the office from when we are with friends and family.

Communication strategies are about reducing friction and achieving the best outcomes for the organization and, where possible, everyone involved. Striving to improve your communication skills continually allows you to advance the organization's goals, while also helping your co-workers achieve their objectives. Happily enough, this also speeds you along your career path. That being said, let's explore these four strategies.

Communication Strategy # 1 – Don't Argue with Reality

Arguing with reality—for example, suggesting it "shouldn't" be a winter storm when in fact, it is—never ends well. We cannot win the argument, but we certainly can make ourselves miserable in the process. How often have you thought, "He shouldn't have said that!" or, "She should not have done that," or, "They should have brought me in the loop," etc. These statements are just as unhelpful as trying to convince the sky to stop snowing when you are sitting there in the middle of a snowstorm. Everyone has different communication styles and preferences and thinking that anyone "should" be any different will only lead to frustration and resentment. Accept your observations of these individuals' behavior as reality. They aren't going to change, even if you want to believe they "should." Then you can ask yourself how to manage and adapt to that reality instead of fighting with it, and instantly, your available options will expand.

Communication Strategy # 2 – Expect to Be Surprised

When you expect a conversation, discussion, or meeting to be challenging, you are remarkably likely to get precisely that: a challenge. The reason is simple: you are on the defensive before you ever say a word, and regardless of how you are at concealing your thoughts and feelings, that defensiveness inevitably comes across. Instead, no matter how painful past experiences with a person or group might have been, remind yourself that you do not know what will happen. Expect to be surprised, and you will discover that people may not be as difficult as you had previously anticipated. Even if they are just as difficult as they have always been, you will be more relaxed and, therefore, more able to adapt and respond to what they say instead of reacting and feeling triggered or upset.

Communication Strategy # 3 – Find the Fear

This strategy, by far, is my most favorite one! Everyone has something to fear, whether shame, embarrassment, anger, anxiety, losing control, insecurity, vulnerability, etc. Of course, this does not mean you should run up to someone and say, "I bet I know what you are afraid of!" Instead, it means exploring the possibility they might have some specific concerns. This strategy requires empathy, delicate tact, and careful timing. Effectively using this strategy can make all the difference between success and failure when managing a situation or a project outcome.

Communication Strategy# 4 – Explore the Third Truth

You know the old saying that there are three truths: my truth, your truth, and the real truth. In any situation, each of us has our version of the truth—about what we believe and what we want. When those truths conflict, we typically dig in our heels and stubbornly defend our position, especially if we tend to be higher on the competitive scale versus collaborative. This will only increase the level of disagreement and conflict. However, it is best to pause and implement the first three strategies mentioned below.

- Stop arguing with the reality that the other person sees things differently than you do.
- Expect to be pleasantly surprised by how events unfold.
- Seek to understand what the other person might be concerned, worried or fearful about.

We can then open to a range of options that would otherwise be impossible. People are often reluctant to explore the other person's viewpoint (or truth) because they feel as if understanding equates with an agreement. But this isn't at all the case. Understanding is merely understanding; you are still free to disagree. When you take the time to understand the other person's truth, you have more clarity about what's at stake for them, and therefore, you have a greater ability to create a new, more mutually agreeable solution to the issue at hand.

These four strategies build upon each other, and they take practice! The first step is always to be aware of where you're coming from and consistently to ask yourself these questions:

- Are you in an argument with reality?
- Are you expecting the worst from an individual or a situation?
- What might the other person be worried about?
- Can you understand their truth, and therefore, seek to create a third, more compelling truth?

CHAPTER 10

STRESS MANAGEMENT TECHNIQUES

I'm sure you've all heard the term "burning the candle at both ends." Well, just like that candle, we can burn ourselves out physically and emotionally to the point of exhaustion if we don't recognize and reduce the stress in a given situation.

What is Stress

Stress is what happens when the body reacts to any change that requires an immediate adjustment or response. The body will then respond to these changes, either physically, mentally, or emotionally.

Symptoms of Stress

We all react to and experience stresses differently. There are, however, some common symptoms of stress that we all share:

- Difficulty sleeping
- Weight gain or weight loss

- Headaches
- Irritability
- Fatigue
- Nausea
- Feeling overwhelmed
- Sweaty hands or feet
- Heartburn
- Panic attacks
- Stomach pain
- Social isolation
- Obsessive or compulsive behaviors
- Disturbing dreams & nightmares
- Constipation, diarrhea, loss of control
- Reduced work efficiency or productivity

It should be noted, though, that stress is our friend; it acts as a protective mechanism that warns us of danger. It's a natural reaction to the "fight or flight" response. When used at the right time, stress heightens our awareness and improves our physical performance needed in short bursts. However, repetitive exposure to the stress response on our body is proven to lead to long-lasting psychological and physical health issues.

Different Stress Management Techniques & Strategies

Below are tips we can all benefit from doing more of. We can categorize them into three groups:

Action-Oriented – *Approaches used to take action to change a stressful situation, such as:*

- Being assertive – Clear and effective communication is the key here.

- Reduce the noise – Make time to switch off all the technology, screen time, and constant stimuli to help you slow down. Ask yourself, how often do you go offline? For your own sake, it's worth shaking this one up a bit.

- Manage your time – Don't let your days consume you. Before you know it, months will fly by because you're feeling extremely busy. When we take the time to prioritize and organize our tasks, we are creating a less stressful and more enjoyable life. Making time to de-stress is as important as making time for the priorities that cause stress.

- Creating boundaries – Boundaries outline what behaviors we will and won't accept. Boundaries also help to define the time we need from others, space we need, and what priorities we have. Critical to a stress-free life is having healthy boundaries. It is natural for us to respect ourselves and take care of our well-being without questions with healthy boundaries, not to mention how we would be expressing ourselves to others through these boundaries. Sometimes, it is best to just move out of your way and get out of your head. Just take a break, distract yourself. See a movie, take a walk, do something positive that you know will take your mind off things.

Emotion-Oriented: *Approaches are used to change the way we perceive stressful situations.*

- Affirmations & imagery – It is now scientifically proven that increasing positive emotion is brought out from positive imagery and affirmations. When you take a minute out to think of a positive experience, your brain perceives it to be a reality. So, would it not be logical then to replace any negative thinking with positive statements to challenge and change the way you see yourself and experience the world around you?

- Cognitive restructuring – This is a technique where we understand negative emotions and challenge the occasional incorrect beliefs that cause them.

- ABC technique – Created by psychologist Dr. Albert Ellis, this technique uses the letters ABC to define the following: A – the adversity, or the stressful event. B – beliefs, basically how you respond to the event. C – consequences, the actions, and the outcome of that event that are a result of your beliefs. Simply put, the more optimistic your expectations, the more positive the outcome.

Acceptance – Oriented: *Approaches are useful in stressful situations that you cannot control.*

- Diet and exercise – You know this already: you are what you eat. You should be mindful of keeping a healthy and balanced diet. Making simple diet changes, such as reducing your alcohol, caffeine, and sugar intake, is a proven method to reduce anxiety. A great way to reduce stress is exercise.

- Meditation and physical relaxation – Use techniques such as deep breathing, guided visualizations, yoga, and guided body scans. These activities help relax the body.

- Build resilience – This is our ability to bounce back from stressful or negative experiences. In short, resilient people are skilled at accepting that the situation has occurred. They learn what transpired the event, and they move on.

- Talk it out – Don't bottle it all up. Find that person close to you to talk with about your worries and about the things that are getting you down. Sharing worries, indeed, cuts them in half. You may even realize that you might laugh at potentially absurd situations. If you aren't a fan of sharing, that's ok for now; just write them down. It's a great way to release them.

- Sleep – I can't stress this one more. Getting a good night's sleep is vital for recharging and dealing with stressful situations in the best possible way.

Most of our worries do sound a lot less worrisome when we take the time to say them out loud.

CHAPTER 11

ARE YOU CONSTANTLY FEELING OVERWHELMED?

It seems like our lives are running daily at a nearly relentless pace. Add in the personal or family needs, and it's all too easy to feel overwhelmed. When this is the case, it is as if the complexity of the world surpasses the complexity of our mind or our ability to handle the level of complexity for us to be effective. Note, though, that this has nothing to do with how smart we are but everything to do with how we make sense of the world and how we operate in it.

A Vicious Cycle

Have you noticed how our typical response to ever-growing workloads is to work harder automatically? Not only that, but we start to put in longer hours, rather than take a few steps back and examine what is making us do this and finding new ways of operating.

The Impact of Being Overwhelmed

There is a cognitive impact on feeling perpetually overwhelmed. This can range from mental slowness, forgetfulness, confusion, difficulty concentrating, or even thinking logically, to a racing mind or having an impaired ability to problem solve. When we do have too many demands on our mind over an extended period, cognitive fatigue can set in, making us more prone at this point to distractions and thinking less agile. Any of these effects alone can make us less productive and, of course, feeling even more overwhelmed. If you are feeling this way right now, let's look at a few key strategies to try out.

Find the Root Cause or Primary Source

Take a minute to ask yourself, "What's the one thing (or two), if taken off my plate, would make 80% of the stress that I feel right now go away?" Now realistically, we know that you may still need to be responsible for that one or those two things, and you can't take them off your plate, but this question can even help identify a significant source of the stress in your life. If it's a project that's almost done, finish it.

Maybe it's just the actual size of the project or task at hand that's overwhelming. If that's the case, then try breaking it down into more manageable components. Ask for additional resources or negotiate the deadline if you are able, or perhaps all of the above.

Hard-Stop Your Time and Workload

This may involve time-boxing the hours you spend on a task or project. It includes leaving the office at a set time or saying no to work requests outside your normal scope. Saying no to these natural escalations and setting expectations for yourself, to yourself, will create more breathing room for you to focus on your priorities with fewer distractions.

Don't Expect Perfection to Be Perfect

If one thing can lead us to make any task or project bigger than what it should be, it is perfectionism. This is a primary culprit behind procrastination and psychological distress. It's a vicious cycle when things pile up, and the sense of feeling overwhelmed sets in, which can then lead to more procrastination and more feelings of overwhelm.

Ask yourself right now what the marginal benefit would be of spending more time on a task or project. If you answer, "Very little," it's time to get it done.

Recognize that as a human, you physically or mentally cannot do everything perfectly. Sometimes an email will get missed. Believe me, if it's that important, they will drop another one soon enough.

Use Your Time Wisely

First, ask yourself, "What is the best use of my time?" Anything that didn't fall within your answer can either be taught or delegated to others accordingly. Managing selected tasks or projects, sending a proxy to specific meetings, having others take the lead on interviews or initial pre-meetings are perfect examples of delegating.

Don't Fear Your Fears

If you find yourself continuously feeling overwhelmed, it may be the fact that you fear what you think will be the outcome of the task or project if something fell through the cracks or you failed. These assumptions of what the end looks like are not likely 100 percent true. They only occupy space in your brain and need to be identified and debunked as soon as they surface so you can better spend your time focused on the current tasks that need to be completed.

Final Thoughts

Most of us will feel overwhelmed from time to time due to demands on our work or personal lives. Try some of the strategies above to help mitigate the frequency and degree to which we feel this way.

CHAPTER 12

IMPROVING YOUR ABILITY TO COPE WITH JOB DEMANDS

The Workplace has Changed Indeed

I can't help but notice just how much more demanding the workplace has become. Timelines, deadlines, resources, and support continue to shrink while expectations and demands continue to increase. Adjusting to this challenging reality requires one to be very adaptable and incredibly flexible.

Because of this, an ever-growing number of workers are trying various coping strategies to manage the changes and stressors in their lives. The question is, have you developed a routine to ensure your well-being? Are you making use of effective time management and visualization techniques? Have you assessed your level of work-life balance?

If you answered yes to the questions above, then congratulations! Your challenge now is to stay on track.

What to Do

So, what are you willing to do about it? Research has shown that well-being and job resilience are more likely to be part of your reality if you are taking care of yourself physically, socially, emotionally, mentally, and spiritually. That might sound like a lot of work but taking even small steps in the right direction can pay off in the long run.

Make a clear perspective shift and take care of your greatest asset: You!

- Express your need to the person you report to by stating exactly what your needs are and providing an example. Be assertive but respectful, responsible, and honest.

- Address your "challenges" before they become "problems," and divide your time appropriately by prioritizing your job demands.

- Take a proactive approach rather than a reactive one to managing work and life.

- Take short breaks throughout the day to clear your mind.

- Ensure you are getting enough sleep and meeting your nutritional requirements.

- Recharge your batteries by securing time to do something in addition to the work that you enjoy.

- Celebrate your successes!

Making an Improvement

Improvement in time management starts with a commitment to take action and to make changes. There are various techniques for making better use of your time as well as tools to make the task easier. Time management software, daily/weekly agenda planners, and At-A-Glance desktop monthly planners are the ones most commonly used. Do your research and identify the one that fits your situation and personal style the best.

A key element to effective time management is the practice of dividing your work according to you and your employer's priorities. With a shortage of time and more to do on your plate, take time to determine which tasks are both important and urgent. When possible, enlist the aid of other employees when delegating is an option.

TIPS:

- Prioritize your obligations on a scale of 0 (least important) to 10 (most important) and evaluate the level of urgency for each.

- Leave some "insurance" time in your schedule for unplanned activities and unexpected emergencies.

- Get the facts! Half of all worries are caused by people trying to make decisions before they have all the facts on which to base the decision.

Come to your conclusion only after you've received sufficient knowledge. Then, once a decision is made, act on it. Get busy carrying out your choice and dismiss all anxiety about the outcome. When you are tempted to worry about a problem, write out the answers to the following questions:

- What is the problem?

- What is the cause of the problem?

- What are all possible solutions?

- What is the best solution?

Final Thoughts

Once you have all the facts, you can start to develop an "action plan," but for a plan to be effective, it requires a clear goal. Setting realistic goals that can be achieved is essential to the success of goals setting. Use the **S.M.A.R.T.** plan to reduce your stress and to improve your outcomes.

CHAPTER 13

WHEN YOUR EXECUTIVE DOESN'T CARE ANYMORE – DEALING WITH APATHY

For those unsure of its meaning, apathy is a lack of interest, enthusiasm, or concern regarding work tasks and responsibilities.

Working as an executive assistant at times certainly feels as if you are in a maze of mixed signals and hidden agendas. One of the most frustrating signs is when your executive begins to show apathy. When you are in a position where defending your executive's actions or making excuses for their behavior or communication cannot be sustained, it is time to look at ways to maintain your sanity. Here is a list of strategies that may help.

Get Experience

Oddly enough, this is a great time to get to know the details of duties for your benefit. In a way, you can take the reins on specific tasks that allow you to learn more about the business or why your department does what it does for the company. Before you know it, by stepping up, you may hear staff joking that you are the one who runs the show.

Take Responsibility

Good leaders do well by making their staff less reliant on them. They support from a distance to help you grow. Apathetic leaders, though, leave you no choice but to take action, including doing those things outside your daily domain. You have no choice but to work without a net to accomplish tasks knowing the executive will either not know or not recognize your efforts. If your executive chooses not to swim, you have no choice but to avoid drowning yourself.

Don't Slack Off

Time to not follow the leader's apathy. It is crucial that when your executive deflects and hides from daily obligations, you do not let that example rub off on you. Don't use it as an excuse to indulge in your own worst instincts.

Don't Gossip

It is all too easy to engage in conspiracy theories the moment your executive walks into a meeting or an off-site engagement. While this is a time to bond with peers, this is not the course of action you should do. Your integrity is called into question when you partake of "speculation" on your executive's actions. So, while your boss leaves their laptop collecting dust, your response to staff asking questions should reflect a bit more of a smile and a "no comment" than a wordy reply.

Give It Time

It will happen…eventually. Your executive, like yourself, answers to a person(s) above them. Know that your lack of confidence in your executive will not be something you experience alone after a while. Wait it out and hope for the best if you have zero interest in an exit strategy. The background whispers will become a loud roar at some point. Remember that once a year, you must explain your achievements and assertions. It has to be clear that you've done everything you can to achieve your goals. Your executive will need to face the same scrutiny.

Involve Your Executive

Your executive is facing similar issues that you feel over time as well. They may be hurt or disappointed by a promotion passover or peer pressure, or they may just be worn down from the daily turf wars. You may notice their emails are always forwarded and they rarely leave the office. Look for ways to draw your executive out from under the carpet. You are natural allies. You are a team. Capitalize on that by approaching your executive to solicit opinions on meetings. Increase their comfort level to maneuver them into a position of contribution.

Don't Poke the Bear

Do not question your executive's conduct when apathy sets in. Your executive has one primary concern, regardless of what is going on. That concern is collecting a paycheck. Anything threatening that will backfire on you. Your executive may feel cornered and lash out at you. You may be witnessing their personal attacks, dirty politics, etc. If someone has done this already, your poke may make you look like a troublemaker. Yes, you have the guts to "go there" and express what the team feels, but this will not end well. It's a tough spot to be. Your executive's superiors only care about numbers, and you may be viewed as a snitch or a complainer. Human resources, when push comes to shove, is inclined to side with management, regardless of your documentation. No matter what, you may be branded as someone who does not play well with others and can't work out your issues. Biting your tongue may be your only option for now.

Give the Benefit of the Doubt

Take a step back and look at the situation with a fresh set of eyes. The frequent quiet phone call may be a case of asking a mentor(s) how to deal with a current issue(s). The closed-door sessions may be their new way to "hunker down" and get business done. Closed doors can also mean setting a significant strategy to move the business forward in a big push. It could be the superiors to your executive dragging their feet and not giving your executive ample room to make things happen. Don't always look for the worst in a situation. It is easier to invoke negative thoughts than positive ones. Hoping for the best in people is okay to do. Yes, you may have doubts, but be aware of an automatic reflex to distrust, as it will make matters worse.

Build a Network

Collateral damage—we all know it has happened on many occasions where the executive assistant suddenly leaves at or near the same time as their executive was relieved of their position. The last thing you need is to be associated with a lightweight leader, as viewed by their superiors. If you feel your executive's apathy will affect you in the wrong way, carve out your own identity. Make personal connections with peers. Look for opportunities to work on projects to build out your influence within your department. Keep moving forward, producing in whatever capacity of work you can. Given enough time, you will elevate your performance away from your executive to be seen as outside their circle.

Don't Dwell

Ok, so you see things aren't perfect. You have issues with how some things are run. Your boss sends mixed messages; the staff does more than usual. Well, that just shows you are like 99% of all of us. Take comfort in the fact you are in a lousy situation with good company. There is hope, and with that, do not give up.

CHAPTER 14

WHAT YOUR EXECUTIVE ISN'T TELLING YOU

There are all sorts of underlying expectations for an executive assistant. The most common one is your executive expects you to read his mind! I am sure that one's not surprising to you. Your executive forgets to mention plans are changing or forgets to copy you on a request, yet he expects you to anticipate changes and adapt to them quickly.

To earn your executive's respect and appreciation, you must know the underlying expectations of you that your executive will never say.

Here is what your executive is thinking, and what you can do in response:

- *Be loyal to me.* Make your executive feel that you are his or her most prominent advocate. You believe in their work and in the direction of their leadership. When your executive believes you are loyal, he or she is more likely to reciprocate in return.

One key component of this rule is to never leak confidential information. Be the gatekeeper, and never abuse your power.

- *Make me look good in EVERYTHING you do.* Yes, they want to look good in everything you do, from your interactions with external vendors or clients to internal stakeholders and employees. Keep things organized, communicate professionally, dress professionally, and handle interruption respectfully, because everything you do reflects on your executive.

An excellent example of this rule: Disagreeing with your executive in front of their direct report(s), higher-ups, or the team won't cast you or your executive in a good light.

- *I expect perfection.* Even though your executive may not be perfect, they expect you to be. Do that by being ten steps ahead of them. If they are late for meetings, keep them on schedule. If their office is disorganized, you are the neat freak.

One example of this rule: If they forget to review or sign documents or return calls, set reminders for them in their schedule, including blocks of time in their calendar to do those tasks.

- *I am nervous when I walk into a room/event to speak.* Be aware that your executive may be worried about delivering a tough message or trying to solicit audience buy-in for a project or new idea, even when he or she acts self-assured. Look for ways to help and show your support.

Example of how you could help: Maybe help to gather as many facts, details, or information as you can to support the executive to feel more confident when presenting. Follow up with individuals/resources needed to collect the required information in advance to allow the executive time to prepare and practice before their speaking engagement.

INTIUATION AND MIND READING

- *Yes does not always mean yes.* Your executive may agree to things/ideas, etc., but it does not always mean a real yes. That's why you need to choose the time and day to have a critical discussion on items/tasks that you would like to accomplish. What was agreeable verbally might be a no when it's on paper.

> *One way to manage this situation: Gather all the facts and detail the advantages and disadvantages, costs, benefits, and expected results on paper. Provide a copy to the executive and book a time to discuss and obtain the yes that you need.*

- *Let's look at this in a couple of weeks.* It means they are not in a mood to deal with the current task. They are looking for a break, and they want you to postpone this for them until they are either in the mood or ready to deal with it.

> *An example of this: When the executive is not up to meeting with someone or wants to plan an executive dinner, one way you can help is by pushing the dates further out to give the executive a break. Come up with a creative excuse on behalf of the executive to buy him or her time.*

- *Can you get the phone or respond to this email?* You probably are thinking, why they can't answer their phone when they are in the office? Or, how come they don't want to respond to this email? It's because they are avoiding either talking to the person or committing to something.

> *One way to help: The best action to take is to do as they said. Take the call or respond to the email on their behalf. It's one of those intangible requirements of the job to protect their space, and you will help them save face.*

- *Let's do something nice this year for a team event or an executive event*: What he or she means is for you to be creative and come up with something to impress and please the audience (costs may not be an issue here). Your executive may be looking to compete with a past ghost (a tradition or predecessor perhaps), and they feel they need to brand (a.k.a. "prove") themselves as better and to top whatever was done in the past!

One thought on this rule: Don't resist or worry about costs. Just get creative and present your new ideas to get their approval and agreement before you proceed!

- *I don't have an ego.* It's totally opposite as many may have an ego at one point or another. After all, confidence and egos are how most of them got to the top! Watch out for when the moments of the "over-ego" arise. Your role here is to understand the behavior and to identify what's important to them and what they are fighting for.

Some thoughts: Your job is not to point out to the executive they have an ego at play here. Your job is to support them with what is important to them and to help them balance between taming their egos and getting what they want when they want it.

- *You have done great stuff, but there is always room for improvement.* You are great, and they are happy with your work, but they want more to be done, and, they're not too clear about what you've accomplished recently. Help bring clarity to this by providing bullet points of tasks, projects, and items that were achieved throughout the year. Most times, the executive will forget what other tasks an executive assistant does, aside from the apparent core duties of calendar management, expenses, and travel booking.

Additional note on this: Highlight and identify the big projects that you've been involved in or led that have contributed to their successful completion.

- *Why don't you come up with a list of how you see your (EA) role evolving in the future*: This means the executive is putting the ownership on you to improve or develop your role. For the most part, they can't think of areas of growth, learning, or expansion for your position. This could be due to the fact the executive lacks a far-sighted picture for the role, especially if the position is viewed as a junior level one or the executive is new to his senior role.

How to manage this: Take advantage of the opportunity to make a business case to convince them how your role can evolve in helping them become more productive, balance personal and work schedules, and help support and drive accelerated business operations, specifically in process and efficiencies. Your goal is to show your executive how you can be a strategic partner and an office management/team leader.

CHAPTER 15

AN EXECUTIVE WHO CHECKS ON TASKS THAT WERE ASSIGNED TO YOU: HOW DO YOU MANAGE?

For starters, if you find yourself in such a situation, take a moment to breathe and ask yourself a few questions. This will help guide you towards the bottom of why your executive checks on tasks to see if you have completed them. Speaking from my own experience, I must say it was hard for me at first to understand. I worked with someone who not only checked on tasks to see if they were completed, but they kept on accepting meeting invites and booking meetings on the side even though that was my role as their support. It was more than trust.

The executive at the time lacked the communication, and at times, he barely shared any updates and kept all the information to himself. You know, as I do, that makes doing our job proactively very difficult. With that said, I definitely could not work like that. I felt that I couldn't provide the professional support or put my excellent skills to use in such an environment.

So, I decided to do a few things in hopes that we could turn this working relationship into a real business partnership.

I decided to schedule a candid conversation with the executive. Let's just say it was no easy task, given I was new in the role, leaving me with little leverage to go on. I now needed to walk in and tell him that this was not a good start for our new partnership. After all, the advice that everyone gives is, "You're new; let your first three months go before you start providing your opinion and rock the boat," or simply put, keep your mouth shut until the probation period is over. No, I couldn't do that. Unfortunately, this approach doesn't work for me, as I like to create an environment that fosters honesty, integrity, and success right from the start. You must be brave to have those difficult conversations right away before any bad habits or wrong expectations take hold.

During our weekly 1:1 meeting, I created an agenda to guide the discussion. I listed my concerns as points and sent it to him in advance to give him a chance to review and prepare his responses, if any.

It was not an "as per usual" agenda. I wanted to convey a polite message to him that I have concerns and to find a way to "get there" on how we could work together to strengthen our business relationship.

The result of this was better than I had expected. The executive shared how he had a bad experience with previous EA support, which led him to lose trust and continuously double-check. The haze began to dissipate as it was becoming clear he had historical issues with prior EAs. This was a good thing. Knowing the root cause always helps.

I knew I had my work cut out for me. I needed to try to get him to relax and trust that I would handle matters. Given the history, this was not going to be an easy task, and as such, it would take a while to see progress. While patience is not my best suit, I needed to expedite the process somehow. I dug deeper to find out all his pain points. I needed to see where promises were not kept and to narrow the gaps to gain his trust. How did I do that? I started by doing the following:

- I scheduled and protected our weekly 1:1 meeting. No matter what, we had to meet to keep the lines of communication open.

- I created a weekly agenda to address pending tasks and to show that his time spent with me was not wasted.

- I assigned tasks that were given to me during our 1:1; this was followed by quick execution and an email update on what was accomplished, what was pending, and what required action from his end.

- Whenever he brought a pain point or an area where he needed help, such as the filing system, booking travel far in advance, or keeping track of important dates and meetings that required follow-up, I was quickly ready to take care of it and provided a sense of urgency to his requests.

- I brought up any meeting conflicts as they arose, so hopefully, he would (and eventually did) stop managing his calendar.

- The 1:1 calendar review was done three months in advance, and any conflict was dealt with on the spot. Even though things always change in any given 3-month period, this gave my executive a feeling of comfort as he began to see my proactive outlook on the business and his productivity.

In short, it was a work in progress to build trust, and it took a long time. There were moments and times where I was quite frustrated, waiting for him to come around. The key was that I needed to be careful in not showing my frustration. Patience was a much-needed practice during that time. If you ever end up in a situation like this, I have put together the best advice I can share in hopes that it will help you manage the situation until trust is built:

- Open communication always; be honest and gracefully candid.
- Be a good listener.
- Be observant; be on the lookout for pain-points so you can fix them right away. Be the hero that saves the day.
- Be reliable and dependable.
- Consistency is a key (do what you say you will do, right away).
- Put in time and effort to show interest and care.
- Address gaps and problem solve.
- Be proactive and show initiative.
- Always have a plan; be creative.
- Be patient (you will need a lot of it).
- Hang in… they will always come around.
- Get to know your team members and what they do to help learn the business. It will be helpful to know your environment and those who can be your go-to for resources to get tasks done efficiently and quickly.

CHAPTER 16

TWELVE EMPLOYEE TYPES THAT DRIVE YOU BONKERS

Oh, those employee types that drive you bonkers! Have you ever worked with one, two, or even more co-workers who were downright difficult to manage? Perhaps it was through lack of productivity or it was a personality that made you wonder why he or she was given the role they were in or how they got to that position.

Let's start by examining some of these personality types.

The Entitled: This type comes in two varieties.

> a) Those who believe their skills and knowledge are an absolute necessity to the survival of the department or organization.
>
> b) Those who have been working there for so long that they think they've earned the right to do things on their terms. For the "a" variety you

must assign low-level, must-do tasks to bring them back down to earth. With the "b" variety, you must assign low-level, must-do tasks to show them you are still the boss.

The Connected: Tend to pull their strength from someone above your head. For whatever reason, they are liked and protected. I have worked with one; it was always a pain to deal with them. Unfortunately, it's worse when these employees are not productive, which often is the case. The best way to manage is by documenting their shortcomings and poor performance; if you can produce genuine evidence and supporting facts, it goes a long way.

The Self-Absorbed: The good part for this type is that they are productive; the downside, though, is that they are out for themselves. They are not team players and rarely will help others. They keep their ideas to themselves, and they do not see collaboration as a positive thing. Such a person may have low confidence and a high need for recognition. Give it time and help them share their knowledge with others. There may be an ego at stake here for them.

The Office Gossiper: They are the faultfinder, the friendly one, the hanging-around-cubicles-chitty-chatty one, the overly helpful one and the comedian at the company's expense or other another person. They have a magnetic personality that attracts bitter, disillusioned co-workers and bullies. You will need to move in fast to stop the gossiper from forming a destructive work environment and hurting others who fall prey to those who think everything is a joke or harmless.

The Delegator: This personality type likes to free themselves from tasks they should be doing. They are the lazy ones. They delegate the tasks they dislike and busy themselves with "pretend" or less involved/targeted tasks to show they are

THE ELEMENTS OF TOXIC WORK ENVIRONMENT

contributing while sending mixed messages to others of what their role truly is and what they are involved in. To manage them, you will need to communicate clearly defined duties/tasks, expectations, and accountability to the assigned tasks they are given.

The Busy Bee: On the upside, they are very productive; however, on the downside, they can get overwhelmed, overburdened, and stressed by taking on more than they can handle. This personality type tends to see their value and worth by taking on more tasks, getting involved in all sorts of projects, and helping here and there, to the point they feed off that busy, chaotic schedule. To manage this person, assign tasks that are longer-term to keep them busy for a while. Check on their workload to adjust whether they can handle the amount. Having a defined clear picture of what projects are important, how they positively impact the overall picture, and how they contribute to the outcome will help the busy bee to stay grounded and focused on one primary task at a time.

The Self-Centered: Everything they do revolves around them. They love to talk about themselves, and they lack awareness outside themselves. They won't go out of their way for anything or anyone if it's inconvenient. For the most part, they take more than they give. One way to manage them, perhaps, is a reward system or an agreement of some sort. You provide something they value; they return the favor as such. Sometimes, you might have to bite the bullet and listen to their story of glory to get them to complete a task for you.

The Pusher & The Bully: By far, they are the worst. They create a hostile work environment. No one wants to work for or with them. Most employees try to avoid them, which does not help the situation. This personality type accomplishes their work by pushing, bullying, and forcing others to conform to their way of doing things on their schedules. They dismiss anyone who tries to delay them from their mission or have a different opinion or idea. They resort to coercion and force to get their way. One way to manage this person is to surround them with staff who have an equal or greater knowledge of the tasks to be completed. Ensure they are with charismatic team players and collaborative individuals. Put a few of those around them to force the bullies to play nice.

The Happy Go Lucky, All Out Helpful: Those types are always happy, smiling around the office, all-out helpful, showing up in your space all the time wanting to help you. You find them everywhere, and you can't escape them. They will water your plant and pick up coffee for you. Heck, they will talk to your boss on your behalf. You begin to wonder what their job is. Be wary as they are the meddlers. How do they have so much time on their hands to be available for help to everyone? These types enjoy being well-liked and depended on. To keep them at a distance, give them tasks that seem important to you and explain that you are in dire need of their help and see them go for it. That should buy you some time and distance. Be strategic on things you ask them to help you with.

The Difficult, It's Not My Job: Those are hard-shelled ones. They don't like to get involved or help others. They love their routine job; they want to do just enough for the pay. Most days, they enjoy being left alone with no one to disturb them. To manage them, you have to get them interested in being involved. Play on their strengths. Find what they are best at and ask them for their expertise. Let them know that tasks for the project can't succeed without their expert knowledge. Explain the big picture, that they will be involved in the success of the team/project etc.

The Disorganized: They will claim they never got the invite and never got the email. These will blame circumstances or, worse yet, others for missed deadlines or targets. They will claim they only receive information at the last minute and need to work magic to complete the assignment. Blaming co-workers' time management skills is an often-used excuse here. Time management courses are helpful here regarding their overall workload. Coaching on managing their email and calendar may help. You may have to remove some tasks and slowly add them back as progress is made. Weekly check-ins and regular follow-ups are good.

The Seasoned Long Termed: They claim, "that's how we've always done it." Their currency is information, and they will use it to maintain a perceived "too important to lose" status. They will play down new ideas in favor of sticking to the current process as it requires less effort. They love to say, "If it's not broke, why fix it?" Routine is very much in their wheelhouse. Try to get their involvement by "secretly" introducing them to new projects or changes. Let them know they will be instrumental in the success and training of other employees.

We have all worked with one or more of these personality types. Finding ways to deal with and manage them will ease those stressful and trying moments when you interact with each one. I have personally worked with all the above personality types. You will find them in every organization, and unfortunately, a few will exhibit more than one type (for example, Disorganized and Long-Termed together). However, it is from painful learned experiences that I can finally say I have smartened up and have begun to find common ground to be able to work with them for my peace of mind.

CHAPTER 17

WARNING SIGNS OF BULLIES AND BAD BOSSES

The primary reason people leave a job is because of either a mismatch in culture or a boss who drives them up the wall. You'll never know exactly what it will be like to work for your potential boss until you have the job. In some cases, you might not even meet your hiring manager until your first day. Hopefully, it will help to look at clues to gather as much information as possible.

Do:

- Pay attention to how the manager treats you throughout the interview process.
- Research the manager, and if possible, find former employees to ask for their perspective.
- Request (if possible) to meet with potential colleagues and your potential boss.

Don't:

- Ignore your gut instincts about the manager as you go through the interview process.

- Ask direct questions about leadership style; you're unlikely to get an honest answer, and they might signal that you don't want the job.

- Neglect to look up your potential boss's social media profiles.

Signs and Red Flags to Pay Attention to:

Pronouns Matter: If your interviewer uses the term *you* in communicating negative information, such as, "You will deal with a lot of ambiguity," don't expect the boss to be a mentor. If the boss chooses the word *I* to describe the department's success, that's a red flag. If the interviewer says *we* regarding a particular challenge the team or company faced, it may indicate that he or she deflects responsibility and places blame.

The Boss Asks Inappropriate Questions: Do you have children? Would your partner be ok with the hours required to do the job? Any questions geared toward revealing your age or religion, etc.

The Boss Lacks Enthusiasm: You should feel a sense of excitement when you consider working for them. But if you feel like the boss hates his or her job and doesn't care, leave immediately. Chances are the office is full of disengaged employees who are plagued by low morale.

Extreme Friendliness: "It may sound odd, but what should have tipped me off was how nice she was," one administrative assistant said of her toxic boss. "Adults don't want to work for a nice boss. It was a trap I could've easily avoided had I caught on earlier."

Self-Absorption: "If his ideas seem to be more important than finding out about your ideas, or if you provide an answer and the interviewer tells you you're wrong or interrupts with his answer to the question, it may be an indication that he will be difficult to work with," noted one technical support staffer.

Fear Used as a Motivator: Be wary if the response identifies a lack of respect for people. When managers disrespect and distrust others' motivations, they resort to extrinsic means with which to motivate, such as threats, public humiliation, and comments about layoffs.

Defensive Body Language: Watch for constant shifting, avoiding eye contact, or rifling through papers as you talk.

Visual Cues: If your boss scans you from head to waist versus waist to head as they extend their hand in greeting you, they are intuitively sending a message that you are smaller than they are

Disrespectful Behavior: Don't overlook unprofessional behavior

Keep track of how long it takes for a boss to get back to you about the position or how long she waits to respond to your inquiries. If you've given up on a job, for example, because you haven't heard a word in four weeks, and then you suddenly get a call with an offer, take time to think about the position, and review your initial gut responses. Bullies often torment their subordinates by making them wait and managing with a carrot-and-stick approach. While she just may have been too busy to get back to you, this is a sign that you should pay attention to.

Verbal Abuse: Be alert during the interview to overly critical or snide remarks regarding your work experience or the companies you've worked with. Also, take note of any offensive jokes that seem to be made at the expense of other employees.

Intimidation: They use verbal or physical threats to ensure co-workers comply with their wishes. Their tone is overly powerful. Therefore, be alert to any statements, name-calling, or degrading criticism that might imply the boss is accustomed to using threatening gestures or words to control fellow employees.

Sabotaging Employee Reputations

To maintain control of employees and their futures, a lousy boss might blame the employees for issues at work and refuse to let bygones be bygones. They might find ways to punish employees for problems over which employees have no control over or deny recommending them for promotion, training, or a transfer based on some long-ago mistake.

It's important to be aware of a boss who gossips about the work and personal lives of co-workers in ways that make employees appear to be unable to handle their responsibilities. Listen to how they describe the work of your predecessor and if they give credit where it's due, or if they blame them for departmental or company issues. If you speak to co-workers, ask questions to determine if the employees seem satisfied with the boss.

These are a few red flags to watch for during the process of an interview. I have experienced all the ones listed on here throughout my career working for different industries. I am the type of person who has been a people pleaser, which I believe is the downfall that led me to accept jobs in the past that were not the right fit. As I look back, there were warning signs all along.

Had I paid more attention to them, and my gut feeling, problems could have been avoided.

Taking the time to ask questions, preparing for an interview by searching the company, and individual manager, as well as trying to reach your network for any sort of information, could help. In the end, preparing for an interview with a plan to impress your potential employers so you can land the job is a one-sided mentally that will not help you succeed in choosing the right fit or longevity.

It took me painful experiences to realize landing a new job needs to work both ways. The potential employer is not just interviewing me, but I should interview them as well. Sometimes you get carried away with selling skill sets and impressing that you miss the essential steps that benefit you in the long run.

Unfortunately, many people lack experience in interview preparation, especially people who have not been in a position often to look for a job. It's guaranteed you will overlook warning signs if you aren't prepared. You must understand what values, skill sets, and talent will benefit you in the future from accepting the wrong jobs and roles. This will protect you from being in a position where you walk out on the job within a few short months.

My advice to my readers is this: take your time during the interview and waiting process. Pay close attention and don't let external forces guide or rush your decisions. Even with an enticing salary increase or an impressive status and title, there is always a *but* or a challenge behind the lucrative offer.

CHAPTER 18

INTIMIDATION: REFUSING & STANDING FIRM

I am sure we all have encountered them: the people who seem to be in total control. They exude self-confidence and, without intentionally doing so, they intimidate you. Intelligent people don't mean to make the modest ones feel unsmart. Assertive people can't always help it if meek one's fade in their presence. When you must deal with these "favored" individuals, something unpleasant often happens. You lose whatever poise and confidence you thought you had. You back off or act foolishly—quite unlike your usual self. Your positive self-image self-destructs.

How Can it Be Restored?

- Successes: It's essential to acknowledge your accomplishments. Too often, we tend to gloss over our successes and obsess over failures. It's necessary to keep both in perspective to build ourselves up.

- Comparing: This is dangerous territory; don't go there. Each of us possesses a complicated set of strengths and weaknesses. For example, an individual may be more able at numbers and less persuasive with people, but the organization needs both types as both styles get work done.

- Perfectionism: Give that up. A rational and healthy standard demand that you try your best, not that you never make mistakes. You must try to make the best of what you have. Remember that the most elegantly turned-out executives will have days when their hair refuses to stay in place, or a presentation fails to deliver the message intended, or a deal turns sour.

Intimidation by Design

In contrast to no-fault intimidation, there's the deliberate kind. Your manager may use coercive power, or a peer may undermine you. Machiavellian tactics for the person to get what they want by exercising their power of authority and getting ahead (unjust criticism, sarcasm, withholding information, ignoring your ideas) make you feel victimized. What you must do is "out-Mac" your opponent. Some pointers:

- Do some self-analysis. Am I allowing myself to be passive? Why is this person treating me like a doormat? If the individual is on your level, it's vital to assess your role to him or her. See if there is a way to establish some reciprocity between you and some basis for cooperation. As colleagues, you need to interact. How does your work affect the other person's job?

- Bring it out into the open. Unless you confront the intimidator, there can't be any progress. Possibly he/she isn't even aware of the effect on you. But if the intimidation is deliberate, serving notice that you aren't going to be passive could go far in squelching it.

- Learn to be more influential. The best way to counter intimidation is to develop your powers. Cultivate your expertise; the more competent you are, the greater your confidence to deal with those who are intimidating.

- Lastly, when the situation is unsalvageable, the scars will be more significant. It's time to remove yourself from the ugly and move on to a safe harbor.

Final Thoughts

Battling intimidation is particularly necessary for a woman who may face a hostile male environment, or for members of minority groups struggling to get ahead. Wherever there is evidence of deliberate intimidation, it is essential to confront it. It is a risk, but one you must take to achieve real growth.

CHAPTER 19

WORKPLACE CULTURES: TOXICITY AFTER A MERGER

In the past, I worked as an executive admin with a company. During my time there, my company merged with a larger organization. As you can imagine, this made for a rough period for the employees.

That merger brought many changes over the long run, where the workforce turned into a battlefield of built-up frustrations among the employees. The larger company decided to roll out a training program called "One Team" to enhance the merger of the two contrasting cultures. The program describes the principle of "one team," which means to be authentic, to build trust, and to make connections. It's a fun and excellent program that is engaging, simple, grounded, and real. However, I believe to obtain employees' buy-in, change starts from the top. One Team was an odd name for this program, but while many colleagues chuckled, I could see its benefit to our company.

What it Means to Be One Team:

- Doing the best job possible and performing above expectations
- Offering innovative ideas to improve things, having productive work relationships.
- Collaborating with others to make informed decisions.
- Being thoughtful and considerate of others.
- Providing people with support and encouragement.
- Accepting change easily.
- Having a strong desire to learn and experience new things.
- Believing it's your responsibility to "win" the customer.
- Listening and asking questions.
- Consciously making decisions that make good business sense.

How Do You Deal with a Toxic Work Culture?

Culture is the way we think, act, and interact with one another. By thinking about the way, we do things and how we work together, we can achieve more and make the organization an even better place to work. Affecting change starts from the top and trickles down, not the other way around. I have seen in the past leaders expecting the change to begin from the bottom up. In one hundred out of one hundred times, this never works!

For leaders to inspire change, they need to model the change they wish to see in their organization. This is not a task that leaders need to delegate; it's a journey where leaders will need to lead with passion, conviction, and tenacity if they seek a better work culture. Simply put, it takes time and effort to rebuild your company culture.

Thinking Drives Our Behaviors

The desired outcome is that our core values guide our decision making, and best practices come to life through one team. When people show authenticity, they build trust with each other and make qualified connections. Thinking drives our behaviors, which is the result of our thought habits and thinking. A win/lose mentality creates a win/lose behavior. Insights help to change your thinking, which in turn helps to change your life. When one focuses on being a "single team," one will focus on high priority items in life, at work or in meetings, and the question becomes, what is the most valuable use of my time and energy?

There is a rationale behind the reason for the changes. Once people in the workplace practice becoming mindful and aware of their behaviors (resulting from their internal thoughts and habits), it will help provide insights into how that affects their mood and the way they see everything. The goal is to be aware of our filters and shed some light on our own biases, whether we are acting consciously or unconsciously. Discrimination is real, and we all play a part in it whether we cover it up with our political correctness or lack thereof. What shadow do we cast? Who we are and how we carry ourselves influence all those who look up to us, at work, and home. Not just what we say, but even our mood impacts those around us.

What is The Mood Elevator?

These are the feelings we experience based on our thinking. The mood elevator is the level/state your mood is at (listed below). Lower levels are less effective and reliable; upper levels are more positive and resourceful. Lower emotional intelligence can be found while in lower level mood states.

A higher level of the mood elevator

- grateful
- wise
- creative
- optimistic
- appreciative
- understanding
- curious

The lower level of the mood elevator

- stressed
- judgmental
- defensive
- anxious
- irritated
- frustrated
- angry/annoyed
- insecure

We Must Keep Moving Forward

Today's workplace is different from the workplace of the 1950s. Gone are the days when much of the workforce were male dominant. Organizations nowadays can't afford to be stuck in the past. In an ever-changing environment, we experience more diverse generations entering the workplace. Organizations must be sensitive to the impact of different cultural backgrounds and various generations at changing our existing core values and overall mission. Respectful interactions with each other and openness to learning new ideas are essential. Showing up every day with personal accountability and commitment to our work and our team, taking ownership of our output of work and caring enough in doing the right thing for our employees affects the overall organization and our customers. In short, the goal would be leading with excellence together through shared vision and innovation.

It is important to stay curious. We all have blind spots, and nothing is guaranteed as we should rely on the wisdom of our team members for better results. Understanding what shadows, we cast can help reduce outbursts and hostile work environments. All styles get results; we must be mindful of how our style shows up when working with one or more other styles that are different than ours. Giving the benefit of the doubt and assuming positive intent is one example of producing a positive and safe team environment that allows for openness, collaborations, and room for mishaps without fear of being penalized. Organizations are encouraged to create and influence a mindset of staying curious. Learning is growing and failing is experience.

Final Thoughts

In terms of culture change, whether it's One Team training or change management, it's the responsibility of the leaders to support and inspire a positive, open, empowered, and knowledge sharing workplace environment. Additionally, this will lend to celebrating growth, adapting to change, and staying curious. The goal is to have the organization adopt and adapt to innovative ways of doing things, to bring forth improvements in the output and the input of job performance with process and efficiency in mind.

CHAPTER 20

MICRO-MANAGING EFFECTS: CAN YOU CHANGE IT?

I once worked in a company as an executive assistant to a senior vice-president. I had to work on projects with one of my boss's direct reports, who, at first impression, was friendly, easy-going, and welcoming. Sounds great, right? Oh well, that didn't last long.

It turns out the VP was newly promoted. Big jump for some indeed. This is true, especially if the leader does not see the employee ready for such a giant overstep into a VP role. In many cases, fast-tracking employees does not allow for learning the managerial skills needed to prepare them.

Anyway, I had to work with the VP on projects that involved conferences, executive meetings, agendas, and executive presentations. The VP had been working in the organization for a while by today's standards. While the VP knew a lot, the VP was a control freak. The VP only cared about their team, but that was a toxic relationship as well.

This VP was one of those who were last-minute with their requests and deliveries. Presentations that generally took a few days would take weeks to pull together, as they had to be a part of all information gathering from other contributing sources and departments, even though they had delegated those tasks.

Every time I had worked with this VP, they drove me nuts micromanaging every move, every email I sent, every task I needed to do. Nothing was ever good enough for the VP because it was not entirely done their way.

The VP's working style affected how I worked and did my job. I was frustrated. I knew how to do my job, and I did it very well. I am quite the capable EA and have never had to deal with being micro-managed or answering to someone other than the executive I supported.

This was a new space for me that brought new challenges and required some learnings from my end. I tried to coach this person politely and to steer them towards building trust between us, that the task would be done efficiently. But that did not last or work well.

One time, the VP snapped at me because they were questioning why I was using a PDF presentation instead of the original PowerPoint. In reality, there was no secret as to why I was using a PDF, but it was a request the VP asked me to do at that point.

Anyway, to make this story short, the VP thought I was using them and that it wouldn't work to run videos or animations. The VP had jumped to this conclusion when the VP was not present during the morning session.

To be honest, I find it very hard to work with people who micro-manage to death, as there is a lack of trust and a whole bag of problems that they are insecure about, and you can't change that. I was silly enough to think I could try; in the end, they wore me out.

For my peace of mind, I decided to find ways to deal with it, given that there was no one on the team brave enough to tell the VP to pull back and to let people do their jobs.

Everyone was walking on eggshells, and they had gotten used to it. When I started to voice my take on it, it caused tension and angered the VP. It came across as though I was undermining the VP and not following instructions. At this point, you are probably asking yourself, what about your executive? Didn't you bring this to the exec's attention? The answer is yes, and my exec told me to ignore the VP, but ignoring does not make the problem go away; my executive just did not want to be put in the middle.

To summarize my findings on this situation, can you change the behavior? No, you cannot. The effect of dealing with a situation like this varies. I felt less motivated, distant, silenced, and frustrated. I was also angry because I felt insulted that my knowledge, experience, and skills did not matter. I felt that because I was new to the organization and had not put in the time, I had no say, and there was no place for new ideas. My original ideas were rejected and stifled every time.

How do you manage in such a toxic environment when changing jobs is not an option for the time being? Well, you are in luck, because I am about to share a few tips with you that might be helpful. It worked for my peace of mind. The situation did not change, but my way of thinking did.

- When a task is handed over by a micro-managing person, accept it graciously and be prepared to ask questions. It makes them feel important. It's a good start to keep them at bay.

- Re-phrase back to them what the task was because it makes them feel in control.

- Commit to a time when you will update them and how you will update them.

- Copy them on all your email communications, even the silly ones (they want to be in the know; it's ridiculous, but just do it for your peace of mind).

- At some point, you might feel like a two-year-old, reporting, asking permission to send something or to change a word in email communication, or even to choose a food menu for catering. God forbid you do that without letting them know if something goes wrong. It will be your fault, so, you better run the big and small stuff by the person. Remember, they want to be in control, so let them.

- Whatever task or steps they need you to follow or do first, just nod in agreement and get it done their way. I know that sounds passive, but believe me, you can't fight against the wave. Might as well join in and hope it will run its course. They will eventually burn out.

- It will drive you nuts thinking about their working style, and some workdays might feel long. Just keep reminding yourself, "This is for my peace of mind." It's a power struggle, so let them have the power and control.

- It's not about you; it's about them. They are overcompensating for their insecurities; don't put that baggage on you.

THE ELEMENTS OF TOXIC WORK ENVIRONMENT

- When all else fails, get through the day, and get home. Have a drink of wine to relax and forget (it does not make the problem go away; it's for humor).

Lastly, as a reminder, they will burn out from their actions as they want to keep their hands everywhere and juggle so many balls at the same time. It is next to impossible to run a successful team in that manner. There is always an end to something, whether you change jobs moving on, or wait until they burn out. Your executive will step up when it truly affects their success. Until then, unfortunately, the pattern most likely will remain unchanged.

RESOURCES

EMAIL UPDATES

Let us keep in touch – to get updates on new blog posts, books, free resources, speaking events, or monthly encouraging newsletter.

Subscribe to my email list at:

https://amalcandido.com/index.php/blog/

CHECK OUT MY COACHING SITE AT:

I love to meet new people and build connections, whether you are looking to connect or looking for a coach to encourage and inspire you to achieve the personal and professional growth that you are looking for, I would love to help support you in your journey.

https://www.amalcandido.com

FREE RESOURCES OR DOWLOADS

https://amalcandido.com/index.php/resources-to-download/

Amal has an associate degree in travel counselling, and she is a certified administrative professional in organizational management and human resources management. Originally, she started her career in the travel and hospitality industry in 2000. She worked in various roles within the industry such as passenger service agent, front desk agent, switchboard, market coordinator, guest relations, and reservation agent for nine years. In 2009, Amal made the shift to working in the corporate financial industry, building her experience from the ground up working as a receptionist/admin assistant in various contract roles. Since then, she has held an executive assistant role, moving, and serving within different departments in the financial industry until 2018. In addition to her past work portfolio in retail, travel, hospitality and the financial industry, she is currently working in the legal sector, learning and gaining new insights, while building and adding to her diverse work experiences and supporting the c-suite executives of the firm. In her spare time, Amal enjoys blogging, yoga, meditation, books and investing in her professional development.

Also, by
Amal Candido

Authentic Leader

Authentic Leader book is for individuals who are looking to gain some insights and learnings from real-life story-telling experiences. It is loaded with tips, advice, and sharing of scenarios in real-time. If you want to improve in your role by learning from other people's experiences, mistakes, and observations, then this is the book for you. With a refreshing, authentic, and honest take on leadership, leading, and managing, the author serves up 19 bite-sized chapters full of tips, real stories, and sage advice.

Executive Assistant's Guide with Soul and Faith

The author shares real-life experiences in this guide, followed by tips and advice shared at the end of each chapter to maintain focus while eliminating the noise. The author believes that to rise above challenges, one must have a clear understanding that we are all working toward the same goals and applying the golden rule of treating all as you would like to be treated in order to gain further insights in succeeding and understanding your role as an executive assistant.

Love, Faith and Mercy

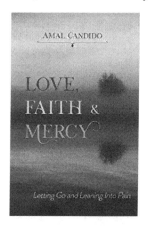

The author's liberating life story about loss, falling, loneliness, making mistakes, and facing hurt shows these can be our greatest calls to courage, forgiveness and living a wholehearted life as spiritual beings. The important lessons involve imperfections, worthiness, strength, and faith and how these lessons connect us with our authentic self, humanity, and each other.

www.amalcandido.com

Printed in Great Britain
by Amazon

24807823R00075